WHY ?

JOSEH

All rights reserved. No part of this publication may be reproduced, stored in a retrieval system, or transmitted in any form or by any means, electronically, mechanical, photocopying, recording, or otherwise, without the prior permission of the author.

Contents

1. Losing Innocence — 05
2. THE ARMY — 33
3. Another new Beginning — 73
4. Am I Sane? — 87
5. Sai Baba — 113
6. The Dream — 142
7. A Matter Of Trust — 155
8. Cooling Fire — 175
9. Why, Why, Why? — 196
10. Running Away Again — 220
11. This Is Your Biggest Change — 253

To My Mother

As a child, you were all there was.

As a teenager, I resented your faults.

As a young adult, I saw your sacrifices.

As a man, God took away my pain

And I learned to love you.

Foreword

If this book has found its way into your hands or onto your computer screen, take a deep breath, for you are about to taken on a rollercoaster ride. There are dips, bumps and hard turns that you may not be prepared for, however, there are peaks that will surprise and delight.

Were it not for the fact I had met the author, I might have believed that this was book was fantasy, or at least grossly exaggerated. But no, this is an uncensored and miraculous, true life journey.

Born into a difficult and violent family setting, the author has had to drag and fumble his way through circumstances that would push the majority of us over the edge. His courage, persistence and seemingly blind faith are at times hard to fathom, but within these pages lies a deep truth and above all a message of hope.

If you are carrying the burden of ingrained habits and attitudes that no matter how hard you try, you just can't seem to be free from. This story proves beyond all doubt, that anyone can change. In fact, with the right effort, we can all be transformed.

When darkness dominates our lives and feelings of desperation, fear, anger and hopelessness prevail, life stories like this help to remind us that these emotions are merely a passing phase, a cloud that covers the sun. Once we start to look beyond the superficial nature of things, there is a light and joy that underpins everything.

This book is not a spiritual template, but within it you may well find an inspiration that will help you to keep on treading the path you are on, with a belief that everything is unfolding exactly the way it has to.

Jonathan Wilcock.

Chapter One

Losing Innocence

My earliest memory of life is of my father. On that day it had been raining on and off and there was a chill in the air, but that did not stop my sister Margaret and I from playing outside, sheltering in the passage between two council houses when the rain got too heavy. We had just emerged after one shower, when a man in a naval officer's uniform strode past us. I was in awe; he had a white hat with a black peak and a long black coat with gold on the arms. Wide eyed, I asked Margaret, "Who is he?" To my surprise she replied, "That's our Daddy."

We followed him home making sure we were not seen, sometimes hiding just to make sure, but he didn't look back.

We stood outside our home for a while arguing.

"You go in."

"No, you go in."

Then we started pushing each other and trying to twist around so the other was in front as we entered the house. We heard Liam and Mick in the living room, so we headed there first; our Dad had already gone upstairs. A large duffel bag and a suitcase were open on the living room floor and my elder brothers were playing with some wooden spears and a shield. I picked up a strange piece of wood that was bent "What's this?"

Why?

Liam, who was ten, and six years older than me, answered, "It's a boomerang".

"But what do you do with it?"

"Dad said if you throw it away, it comes back."

I looked at it doubtfully; I had never known a piece of wood to do that. I was still holding it when my father came down the stairs; he had changed out of his uniform. Mick and Liam stopped playing and went very quiet, but he went straight out the front door and almost as quickly, they started to play, but not as loud as usual. The atmosphere in the house had changed from loud and playful, to a quiet apprehension. Going to bed that night was different; something had changed.

The following months caused me to have a growing sense of fear; my home was no longer a safe or happy place to live in. Any opportunity to be outside was taken, as my father's moods became increasingly unpredictable; something my older brothers already knew about. He did what I would do later in life; he drank excessively. Maybe for the same reasons I would, to help drown out the world, but he would not have the chance to change, as I would much later in my life.

Saturday mornings he would be waiting with his childhood friend Neil Colins for Sudgie's pub to open; the place was dark brown, stained from years of cigarette smoke and stank of old spilt alcohol and tobacco. When the doors opened, the bar top would already be stacked high with trays of cheap wine, it wasn't bought by the glass but by the tray. Within minutes, smoke hung like a thick cloud as the men tried to drink as much as they could before throwing out time.

As the drinks flowed, so would people's tempers, but my father could handle himself, having trained as boxer when he was a teenager. He was known for having a bad temper; a local policeman once said to my eldest brother after my father had died.

"Are you Liam Hempsey's son?"

"Aye", replied Liam.

"Yer old man wus a hell o a fighter, we didn't like tay lift him when he hid a drink in im caus he always gave as good as he got."

That kind of summed him up; he was not afraid of fighting, even with the police.

By three in the afternoon the bar would close, some men were helped, out some were carried out bodily. My father would head home and sleep in the living room. If he woke early enough, he would go back out drinking, spending money that was needed for food.

Around five, my mother would call us in for food. The living room would stink of alcohol from his breath, he had only been back from the ships a short time, but we all knew we would have to be very quiet for fear of waking him.

As the night drew in, our home would be very quiet. Five children and one adult sitting huddled together around one seat in the living room, on one side an open coal fire and on the other my sleeping father.

"Yous must not wake your Dad", Mum would whisper to us.

Why?

She had more reason to be afraid. When he was drunk, he had a very short temper, even shorter than usual, and he would just as easily beat her.

If he did woke too early, he would go into a rage, punishing whoever woke him, or if he slept to long he would beat my mother for not being able to go out again for some more drink. She knew that would happen, but she also knew that we would go hungry if he spent all his pay on drink.

As I look back on my few memories of him and on the stories told by my two elder brothers, I realise that he was a man with two extreme personalities. One was a very charismatic person who would do just about anything for people outside his family; who seemed to love children, knew how to make them laugh and could be generous and considerate.

He was always well dressed and at times immaculately so. Mostly with clothes supplied by his mother, but unfortunately which were paid for from the child benefit that my mother should have received from the government, which, due to borrowing had fallen under the control of my grandmother.

We, his children, were dressed in second-hand clothes from our cousins.

The other part of my father's personality, was a weekend drunk who chased women and beat his wife and children. We would never know which side of his personality would be coming home after work or the pub.

Losing Innocence

This aggressive man hated weakness in others, which made him highly critical of his children and wife. Liam and Mick told me of an occasion when they had got into trouble fighting and had lost, that my father sent them back out to fight the child again until they had beaten them.

To disobey this order or fail to achieve success would ensure that he would give us a beating far worse than any other child could give. I learned to fear him, not just for the possible violence, but also his aggressive criticisms. He would go into a rage for the most trivial of reasons; many times I was given a slap for simply not closing a door or making too much noise (meaning more than a whisper).

So my family lived in constant fear, always having to tread gently around his unpredictable moods.

At five years old, I was still wetting the bed. My father's way of dealing with that was to taunt me. He seemed to think that humiliation was a good way to cause change in his children. It did not work on me; it only caused me to become introverted.

One summer morning I was coming down the stairs from the bedroom. On nearing the living room, I heard raised voices from inside. Slowly and quietly I approached the partly opened door and peered through the gap, unseen by anyone within. I could see Margaret, my sister, crying. She was standing in the middle of a group of children that where taunting her. My father was encouraging them to call her names for something she had done wrong.

Why?

Because of the narrow angle of the door I could only see Margaret, Neil and my Dad, the gap was too small to see who the others were. My father was kneeling behind Neil encouraging him to call Margaret names. Neil had been worked into such a frenzy of excitement over what he was doing, that he was jumping up and down as he called her names. He had no idea that what he was doing was causing pain to his sister, the only thing that Neil was aware of was that it pleased our father. My younger brother could only have been three or four years old at the time. As I watched, I knew it would be my turn next, and the fear I experienced then is still tangible 30 years later. Like an electric shock so severe I could taste it in my mouth, I ran terrified out of the house. Many other times I was not so lucky. I would have to stand there taking the abuse. I learned that if I showed any emotion at all, it would only make the abuse last longer.

I was also starting to learn that when my father hit me, not show any emotion. To take it, and stand there no matter how much it hurt and not cry, for crying was a show of weakness that only angered my father more. "Shut up or I will give you something to cry about."

I knew that another slap would soon ensue until I became quiet.

In learning how to hide my feelings from everyone. I had found an inner strength that allowed me to stand there, no matter how painful things became. His anger had caused me to become more withdrawn and clumsy, especially when he was around -- the very weaknesses that he hated so much in others.

Until my father left the Navy, Margaret, Neil and I were very close and always played together, but not long after he came back that started to change. I must have been about six years old; I awoke to find the bedroom, which I shared with my three brothers and sister empty. I felt confused and disoriented, as I had never awoken and been alone, there was always someone around.

Neil and Margaret, who were closest to my age, were gone, and so were Liam and Mick.

I quickly went downstairs to look for them, but there was no one there, only silence. My mother was in the kitchen washing clothes. She was looking out the window with a very distant expression on her face. I asked timidly where my brothers and sister were. She told me: "Your father has taken them out."

I can't remember what then happened, as my next memory was of being back in my room, sitting alone, very frightened and crying. The feeling of loneliness was overwhelming, it felt as if every nerve in my whole body was raw; I had been left alone in a room to cry.

Later that night they all returned happy and excited, having had a great day out.

They told me later that our father had awakened them early that morning, telling them to make sure I was not disturbed, and quietly took them away.

It was among one of the many events that started me withdrawing emotionally from people and the world around me. In doing so, it slowly made me feel increasingly alone.

There is only one occasion when my father was proud of me. I had torn my clothes at school and feared the consequence. On the way home I passed a wedding party. In Scotland the family of the bride and groom throw money to children as they get into cars to go to the wedding, a lot of pushing goes on as the children try to get as many coins as possible. I managed to get five pence, a lot of money to a six-year-old in 1970. I thought I could use this as an excuse for my torn clothes, so I told my father that I had had to fight another child for the money. Sure enough, that story made him proud of me. A ripped pair of trousers was a small price to pay for his boy beating another child in a fight.

Other children thought my father was great fun. Often as he walked home from work, a crowd of children would gather around him, laughing and playing with him. He would lift several of them at a time into the air, which they all enjoyed and cried out for more.

I would stand at a distance watching them, wanting to join in, to have the attention he gave so freely to the other children, but I had become too afraid of him. I knew another side of him that was too unpredictable, with the very real and painful risk of rejection, which was enough to make me keep my distance from him. Even when he seemed to be happy.

Many times, my brothers and I had to watch out for him returning from work, so we could warn our mother to put his dinner on the table as he walked in the door.

Losing Innocence

We all knew that if for any reason it was not ready or not good enough, then he would go into a rage shouting,

"Am not eating this shit", as he threw the food and plate at mum. He would sometimes beat mum before storming off to the pub, it seemed that he used food as an excuse to go drinking.

Sometimes she would try to stop him hitting us, only to be hurt herself. The corner of the living room became a place my mother would often cower when Dad beat her.

Not closing a door was all the reason my father needed to go into a rage. I often remember my mother saying,

"Liam, you can't hit children the same way as you would an adult."

He was either not aware of his own strength, or unable to understand the pain he caused his own children. My head would ring from the strength of his slap.

A quiet child already, I became increasingly introverted. Many people said that I was a wonderful child because I was so quiet.

The reality was that I had become so afraid, I was trying to hide. If no one noticed me, then no one could cause me pain, but hiding creates loneliness and loneliness creates depression, a very vicious cycle.

When I was seven, my teacher asked the whole class to do some artwork using polystyrene squares and spaghetti. I painted the background totally black and by

Why?

using the spaghetti I made a single flower leaning to one side, as if it was blowing in the wind.

Some of the pictures were selected to be hung in the local council buildings, including mine, but I refused. Instead I took it home and sat at the bottom of the stairs, just staring at it, crying.

Even at that age, I knew that it represented me and that I felt very alone.

I thought that others would easily understand its meaning just as I had, so afraid of what others might say or think, I tried to hide the picture, along with my feelings of being alone.

My last memories of my father were when I was eight years old. It was a clear and sunny day in late March. My brothers and I had been sent to collect manure from some of the local farmers' fields, without the farmers knowing.

That morning we had been given two pieces of advice.

"If it's got horns it's not a cow, but a bull, so run fast." And "Don't be seen by the farmer, as he might shoot you".

So not being seen became very important that day, but first we had to find the fields that had cows in them.

In the early seventies most fields had a small brick wall around them. We had to crouch low along the walls so as not to be seen, and talk in whispers even though the only living things around were some birds and a few cows.

Neil and I would run into the field to find the cow

Losing Innocence

pats, and shout on Liam and Mick when we had found one. They would run out with a shovel and plastic bag to quickly scoop it up, at the same time keeping an eye out for any possible farmer that might object to having some old dung scraped off the grass. By mid morning we had collected two plastic bags full of dung, which was about all Mick and Liam could carry home.

We arrived home around 2 o'clock in the afternoon, put all the manure in a large drum in the back garden and then mixed it with some water prior to spreading where my Dad's vegetables would be grown.

As we were mixing it, I noticed my father standing by the kitchen door. He had come out to watch – it's the clearest memory of him I have – leaning against the frame of the back door with a can of beer in his hand. I looked over at him as he had started to laugh. Neil had got some manure on his arm and was pulling a disgusted face at it.

I was standing furthest away just behind my elder brothers Mick and Liam, tying to peek between them. It was good to see him laugh, but I still wanted to hide from him, for even when my father was laughing I was still afraid of him.

Suddenly he collapsed just by the kitchen door. Liam and Mick rushed over to help; he was throwing up and could not speak. They tried to pick him up, but only managed to drag him into the kitchen. I looked on in shock as my Dad lay on the kitchen floor with his left arm locked rigid across his body, the fist was clenched, and his left leg was shaking uncontrollably. His eyes were alert, but he was unable to communicate. He had

Why?

lost all his bowel control, peeing himself and kept being sick; his whole body seemed to be emptying itself. I just felt confused and very much afraid. After a short time, one of our neighbours came in, picked my Dad up from the kitchen floor and carried him into the living room. Mum took me, Margaret and Neil into the kitchen. Liam and Mick where left in the living room with Dad, to help clean up the vomit.

Years later, Liam told me that the whole time he was trying to help, our Dad was staring at him, his eyes following his every move.

"His eyes seemed to be pleading with me to help", Liam said.

Even as an adult, the memory still haunts him.

At first Neil, Margaret and I were left in the kitchen, but as the hours passed we all ended up in the living room, watching him, frightened. His breath was rasping and seemed to rattle in his chest. When a doctor eventually arrived, my father was already unconscious. The doctor would not believe that there was anything wrong with him other than that he was drunk, and that a "good night's sleep" was all he needed.

It took our next-door neighbour to convince the doctor that my father had only had one drink that day and that there was something very wrong with him. Reluctantly, the doctor called for an ambulance and then we had to wait several more hours.

Slowly, family and friends started to arrive, but no one spoke to us. All I could hear was whispered conversation, which only seemed to heighten the silence and feeling of tension.

At nine o'clock, an ambulance arrived for my father. Two hours later he died. He had been in a coma for most of the day.

Margaret, Neil and I had been sent to our grandparents' for the night, and the next day Liam and Mick came to tell us that our father had died.

My reply to them was,

"Does that mean Daddy can't hit me anymore?" I was eight years old.

On the morning of my father's funeral we woke to find three inches of snow on the ground, it was very cold, such a contrast to the sunny day on which he had collapsed.

I have been told that I was at my father's funeral, but no matter how hard I try I cannot remember. There is only the feeling of coldness and of wanting to be sick. It is one of those many memories in my life that are lost to me.

People turned up at his funeral by the busload — a mark of how respected and well liked he was.

Several days later when I returned to school, the teacher told the class that my father had died and that we should say a prayer for him. I had to bow my head very low so that no one could see the smile on my face. Even now I am not sure whether I was happy because he had died or because I had become, for a moment, the centre of attention. Either way, both were a sad indictment of how I was thinking as an eight year old.

Why?

My mother had a traumatic time with my father, for she was often the target of his cruel side. It seemed to me that the only escape that she had, was to hide in romantic books, always reading. I also found out many years later that my mother often prayed that my father would die, as it seemed the only way out of the painful situation she was in. So when he did die, she then in part blamed herself, often having nightmares where she would wake up screaming in terror, as my father tried to take her with him.

After the funeral, we began to spend a lot of time at my mother's parents, as Mum took on several part time jobs, but she was still having difficulty making enough money to feed us, often going without a meal herself. Several times, the Social Services turned up at our door at night after having received complaints that she had been neglecting us. After that, she would point at occupied cars that sat on the road outside the house, often for several hours late at night, saying with some bitterness,

"That's the Social Services checking that I don't have another man in the house."

Maybe it was a bit of paranoia, but there were only two people that owned cars near our home, so anything strange was noticed straight away. Mum always blamed Dad's family, although we never really knew who had been making the complaints. The stress for her had become so bad that she did consider putting us in a care home. Two teenagers, three small children, several part time jobs and a home to keep, were all taking their toll on her. Her best friend, Betty Taggert, spent a lot of time helping mum. Betty lived in the flat below my grandparents, so when she stayed late, her parents' lodger, Benny McKay, came to our home to pick her up. He was always smiling and trying to be helpful, and although he was a taxi driver, he never charged Mum or Betty. Benny was the double of the actor Sid James from the old 'Carry On' movies; a face that some would say had a lot of character, or just old way before his time.

I was nine or ten when Mum and Benny started to have a relationship. It also happened to be about the same time as mum started to take legal action against the ship yard that Dad worked in. It seemed that several days before he collapsed, he had been struck on the head by a scaffolding board, which was thought to be the reason he died of a massive brain haemorrhage. In other ways life seemed to be settling down – no violence, no fear. I even began to miss not having a Dad. It's surprising how often other children said "my Dad this, my Dad that", but I couldn't. I went down to the graveyard a few times by myself and stood looking at his stone above his grave thinking, "Why, why, why". I would ask myself the same question almost thirty years later in India, and would not like the answer.

Not long after Benny moved, in he showed Liam and Mick what he was really like. The three of them were walking along a road near our grandparents' home, when unexpectedly he crossed the road. Liam and Mick continued walking on the same side, as they saw no benefit to going on the other side. Benny strolled

Why?

up to a man that was walking in the opposite direction and without any warning, head-butted him so hard that the man was lifted off his feet. As he lay on the ground unconscious, Benny casually walked back across the road without giving the unconscious man a second glance. Liam and Mick where shocked into silence, Benny did not even attempt to explain what he had done; it was not something my brothers wanted to ask him about.

Benny was not someone I came to look upon as a father figure. At first he seemed to be charming and helpful, but something was never right. It was not long before he really started showing the rest of us what he was really like.

Like my father, Benny had a drink problem and was often violent, but his violence was different. He seemed to take pleasure in hurting people, even children. He would slap us for anything, especially when there were no other adults about. Other times, his threat of violence was more subtle.

One Saturday afternoon, my mother, Neil, Margaret and I were in town with Benny. A man, who was a friend of the family, came over and simply said, "Hello Lena" to my mother.

This was all that was needed. Benny lost his temper and stormed off in a jealous rage. The look on my mother's face made it clear she was afraid.

When we returned home later that day, he was there in a foul mood and we all knew that he would take it out on us. We went into the living room, only to become cornered as Benny started to rant about my mother talking to other men. He kept moving from the living room to the kitchen incoherently ranting. On one visit we heard him rummage around in the kitchen drawers, I could hear pieces of metal being shoved around, then he stormed into the living room brandishing a knife.

Mum kept saying, "Please Benny, stop."

"Please stop."

"Benny Please!"

He waved the knife threateningly at Mum, she raised her arm only for Benny to slash at her, cutting her arm. Mum moved away from Benny, taking Margaret, Neil and I as far away from him as she could in such a small space. We were now in the far corner of the living room.

Mum was trying to put her arms around all three of us, while also trying to stop the blood running down her arm. She was crying. Benny kept walking from the living room to the kitchen with the knife ranting, but he now seemed to have forgotten about everyone. Whatever world he was in, he was now there on his own. We were now just witnesses to his madness, standing afraid in a corner waiting for him to calm down.

It is difficult to describe the feelings of fear and helplessness that happened to me when faced with such madness, repeated week after week. Watching a grown man act in such a way, would for me, have a deep and profound effect that would resonate through a large part of my life.

Why?

Another Saturday I watched him having the DTs, or maybe he was on some sort of drug. He was cowering on the living room floor waving his arm in front of himself, repeatedly saying in a strained whisper,

"Get away. Get away ", as he crawled into the same corner of the living room he had forced us into.

I have never been able to forget the look of fear on his face, or his hoarse plea for the nightmare to stop. I stood about three feet from his leg, side on, so I could run if things turned bad, and Margaret was several feet behind me.

Although we were both frightened, we tried to reassure him:

"Benny there's nothing there, there's nothing to be afraid of."

He wouldn't stop, saying,

"Get away. Get away ", while still waving his arms at nothing.

"Benny what is it?"

He would not answer, it was as if he could not see or hear me.

I tried asking again what it was he was seeing, but he would not answer; he just kept waving his arms and pleading, "Get away, get away!"

Eventually he fell asleep in the corner.

Margaret and I sat in the room not speaking, what could we say, how could we explain or understand a grown man cowering in a corner with such a look of fear on his face?

Losing Innocence

I was failing badly at School. The poor, quiet, skinny boy that didn't wash as often as he should have, led to me having no friends, which only led to me becoming increasingly withdrawn.

It was only at the age of eleven that I finally stopped wetting the bed. Unfortunately, as my hygiene was not very good, not surprisingly I had no close friends. I had long since learnt to keep my own company, having found teasing from other children deeply painful.

To watch others being teased made me cringe, leaving me feeling confused. Did other children not understand how much pain it caused? Why did they want to hurt others? I found no answers, so I avoided people as much as I could.

Another cause for stress and embarrassment was that I was about to go to secondary school, and I could still hardly read and write. I had still not managed to get past the first two pages of my spelling book, whereas the other kids in my class had about finished the whole book.

All of this left me with little enthusiasm for life, and I would often think, "Is this it? Is this all there is?" All I felt was emptiness.

My schoolteacher asked the class one day, "How old would you like to be when you die?"

As she went around the class asking each child, their answers were "60"; "70"; "80"; "90". When it came to my turn to answer, I had had some time to consider what to say.

"18", I said.

Why?

There was a deafening pause, then the teacher moved on to the next child.

My thinking was that at least school gave me something to do, but after that I saw no reason for anything. What was the point to life? All the adults I knew seemed to be unhappy; life for them seemed to be a constant struggle. There was nothing I wanted to be or do, nothing inspired me to want to do anything with this life. I had no way of expressing what I felt. I had lost trust in everyone, all I could see was a constant grind, but for what? There seemed to be no point to life.

At home, things were getting worse. I would lie awake most nights, nervously waiting for Mother and Benny to come home. I had come to think that is was normal to hear raised voices coming from the living room at night. It took me a long time to realise that at first my father, then Benny, would be arguing almost every night, sometimes violently.

The worst nights were when Mum and Benny went out, as alcohol would bring out Benny's jealous nature. I would go to bed about nine, but could not sleep as I lay awake waiting on them coming home. Time would slip by slowly and on the long summer nights, darkness would creep into my room a long time after I had gone to bed. One of the nearby streetlights would come on and I would watch the shadows of a nearby tree move across the bedroom walls. On windy nights, as Winter drew in, the bare tree's branches became spindly fingers that seemed to claw over the walls as I waited nervously for the sound of someone walking along the path. The distinct sound of steel heeled shoes crunching on the loose tarmac path outside my home, would warn me that someone was coming. Each time I heard someone approaching I would tense, then relax as they walked past, trying to figure out if it was one person or two and feeling relived if they walked passed. My heart would sink if they turned off the tarmac onto the concrete path that led to the front door. The sound of their shoes would change and become louder, and my stomach would twist, for I knew that the moment they entered the house they would be arguing, or worse.

From my bed I could hear the shouting and banging, which often went on for several hours, I would lie awake listening, helpless, unable to do anything about it. If the police came, it stopped for a time. They would take him to the end of the avenue, only for him to return a short time later.

I felt that I had no one I could trust in, so I started to pray at night, especially when there was an argument, in the hope that it might stop it, but it didn't. After a time I went from praying, to pleading with God to take me away from what was going on, silently crying myself to sleep as I pleaded.

"Please take me away from this",

I even tried to bargain with God.

"If you take me away from this life I will go to pray every day."

Why?

Even God seemed to ignore me. So I gave up praying for change, believing that God was too indifferent to be concerned with me. I still believed in God, I just stopped trusting him. That would change some twenty years later.

Things did improve financially when I was about 13. My mother received some money from the company that my father had worked for. The court believed that a scaffold plank had hit him on the head several days before he died, causing the brain hemorrhage that killed him.

In other ways, things got worse. Liam and Mick moved out, Liam first because he got married. Mick followed a short time later, because Benny really started to make his life a misery soon after Liam had gone.

Most nights my mother would go out with Benny, which always seemed to end in arguments and violence. The stress that I was under was causing a physical problem: My hands and my feet came out in a rash, the skin cracked and open cuts appeared, even the doctor said it was stress, but the treatment was cream.

Around the time I was 14 - 15, Benny was finally thrown out. Margaret, Neil and I had been listening to an argument from our bedroom; we sat quietly looking at each other. We heard our mother cry out in pain several times, which culminated with a loud bang and our mother's cry became more like a whimper; we could hear her tearfully pleading with him to stop. It was too much for the three of us. Without saying a word to each other, we quickly got dressed, then stood at the top of the stairs and shouted down.

"Mum are you all right?"

Benny angrily came to the bottom of the stairs and shouted,

"Get to bed now!"

"How is our mother?"

"Shut up and get to bed."

We just stood there, very afraid, asking again.

"How is our mother?"

Then our mother came into view, there was blood all over her face and she was still crying.

"Go to bed, it's okay, go to bed", she said.

We could only look on at her in stunned silence. Too afraid of Benny to go down to her.

"Throw all your clothes down the stairs now", Benny demanded in a threatening voice.

He wanted to make sure we could not leave the house. At first we ignored him, but he became more threatening, then mum said,

"Please do as he says."

We moved into the bedroom whispering to each other,

"If we throw everything down stairs we can't go for help", said Margaret.

"I know, hide some", I said.

We did not have many clothes, so we hurriedly gathered some bits and pieces and threw them to the bottom of the stairs.

Why?

We decided that we had to go get some help from our elder brothers. We could not get past Benny to get to the front door, but we knew we had to get out of the house somehow.

"Well, I can jump out of the bedroom window into the back garden", said Neil.

We went to the back bedroom and Neil climbed out onto the ledge and jumped.

"Come on Joe, it's easy", Neil said in a low voice.

I looked down, the garden was white with snow and in the darkness, shadows filled the area that I would be landing in, which made it seem an awfully long way down from the second floor window. Neil called for me again but there was no way I was going to jump.

"Hurry up Joe."

"No, I cant", I replied.

"I'll climb down the drainpipe form the bathroom."

As quietly as I could, I climbed out of the small bathroom window and made my way down the pipe. About half way down I heard Neil say in a low whisper,

"Stop".

I looked down and froze, just a few feet below me was Benny, his face pushed up against the kitchen window, he was peering intently into the snowy darkness of the night. I could see him so clearly; the light from the kitchen framing his head in the small window. He kept looking left and right obviously wondering what was making noise from the back garden. I held my breath as I half expected him to look up at any moment, then he turned and disappeared. Afraid, I stayed where I was until I heard Neil give me the all clear and I slowly came down the rest of the drainpipe. It was now after around two in the morning. Benny had been arguing for over two hours.

We started the two-mile walk to our brother Liam's house. It was bitterly cold that night, the snow must have partly thawed the day before, so as the night drew in, the temperature dropped well below freezing, causing a layer of thin ice to form, which made a loud crunching sound as we walked. It was the only noise, no cars, no people only the 'crunch, crunch' as we walked in the biting cold, which we felt so intensely, because we had thrown our heavy clothes down to Benny. It did not take long before we started to suffer from the cold. We had stopped talking, concentrating only on where we were going and trying not to think about the cold that surrounded us, or how deep it seemed to have entered our whole body. When we finally reached Liam's home we were almost blue with the cold, a chill seemed to have entered the core of my body.

We banged on the door for some time before we managed to wake someone. Mick answered, he had been sleeping on Liam's couch some time, having had to leave home because of the constant violence that was being directed towards him and Mum. He had tried to tell our relatives what was going on but, Mum being ashamed, had denied it, so Mick ended up being branded a liar.

Why?

We told Mick and Liam what had happened; they decided to deal with Benny themselves. The police had been called so many times and all they ever did was take Benny to the end of the street, tell him to calm down and let him go.

Mum stayed with Liam and his wife for a time so that Benny could not find her. After school we would go to Liam's home, have some food, then later on we would go home with Mick. We eventually heard that Benny went to work in Germany. Mum moved back home and so did Mick, and our lives became more peaceful.

I was not to meet Benny again until the age of nineteen; I was on leave from the army and was drinking at a local social club. The bar was large and poorly lit, but Benny still managed to catch my eye the moment he came through the door. At first I did not recognise him, as he was at the other end of the hall. It was just a man moving rather quickly on a pair of crutches that caught my eye. As he moved closer to the bar, he had to weave between people and seats, but he had still not slowed down. Then I finally recognised him. I stood totally motionless by the bar; his movement towards me became everything, seeing so clearly his face. I was transfixed by this man, who seemed to have grown old in such a short time. As he moved closer to me, he passed the man that had said "hello" to my mother so many years before. The man looked at me, then turned back to Benny and said something that I didn't catch, but the look on his face was unmistakable. He then looked back at me with a smile that was empty, I knew whatever he had said was not nice. It was only as Benny was in front of me that he recognised me.

"Ah, hello, Liam."

I was surprised at the sound of my own voice, which came out clear and strong with no emotions.

"My name is Joe."

The lines around his eyes seemed to become hard as I said my name; he then just turned and walked away without a second glance. I watched his back until he exited by a nearby door to another part of the bar.

The moment I had recognised him, I felt a tremendous shock go through me, as I watched him draw closer and heard him being ridiculed, the shock was replaced by sadness. He just seemed a sad, unhappy old man. I was surprised at my own feelings, there was no anger for the years that I was forced to live with his violent nature, I felt only a deep sense of sadness.

Years later, I came to understand that the sadness was really a glimpse of what I was carrying within, a legacy born from the time he had lived with my family. The feelings he helped generate as a child would flow like an undercurrent, tainting all other experiences until I was in my thirties, when I was given a painful reminder of what was hidden within and an opportunity to have it removed.

I have no memories of Benny being violent towards me, but in 2001 my brothers and I had one of our very few get-togethers. After some alcohol had flowed for a while, the past came up. Neil surprised me by saying,

Why?

"He used to hit me, but he beat you all the time".

All I can remember is that if he lifted his hand while I was near, I would flinch away from him. If there were others around he would lean over me and stare down with a bland expression and say,

"What's the matter with you?"

I always remember it as an unspoken threat, which I was too afraid to answer.

Liam also surprised me by saying that our father seemed to be mellowing just before he died. Other things were said and some deep emotions were touched on that night, but those are my brothers' stories and not to be told by me.

Why?

Chapter Two

The Army

By the time I left school at 16, I had opened up a bit and allowed some friends in, but now I had to get a job. I had no qualifications, I still had difficulty reading and writing and my maths was less than basic. The biggest problem though, was that there was nothing I wanted to do. I aspired to nothing; I wanted nothing. My childhood had taught me to wrap myself in the moment, afraid of the pain the next moment might bring. I was not even aware that I had so tightly clothed myself in fear.

In the early 80's my small town had been hit very hard with a major recession, tens of thousands of men and women had been made unemployed from the local factories and shipyards. My two elder brothers had already got apprenticeships. Mick decided that the best thing for me was to join the army and the only way to do that was to nag, cajole and bully me into going to the Army Careers Office.

The Army

After several months of almost constant intimidation, I decided to go. Mick was only too happy to tell me where the office was and I am sure if I had put it off any longer, he may have dragged me there.

It seemed only to be staffed by one Sergeant, who as soon as I introduced myself, seemed to know of me.

"Ah, you're a Hempsey! You can do the test now."

I was promptly given a piece of paper and pencil and left in a small cupboard-sized room.

It was supposed to take one hour, but the Sergeant gave me a bit more time than he should have. Even with an extra 20 minutes, I still did not manage to answer all the questions. I then stood by the Sergeant's desk as he went over my answers, erasing my incorrect ones then very helpfully telling me the right answers, at the same time correcting my test sheet for me. It was just like being at school! I thought this was normal, standing beside a schoolteacher's desk as my work was corrected. I was not aware that he had taken it upon himself to cheat for me.

A few weeks later, I received a letter advising me to go to the main careers office in Glasgow for another test and a medical examination.

The medical was like something out of an old movie. I stood around in my underwear and was asked to perform some tasks, "Bend over, cough, how do you feel?"

"Fine thanks!"

"Take a deep breath."

It could not have taken more than two minutes before I was being pronounced fit and ushered out the door.

Why?

I was sent to another room, which already had about fifteen other people, each seated at a small desk with some papers on them. This was what I had dreaded, a test.

I took a seat. Just having to look at the piece of paper in front of me caused me to feel ill.

Sometime after the test I was called into a small office, where another Sergeant was sat behind a desk looking at both my test papers. He ignored me as I entered. Without looking at me, he flicked his head at the seat in front of his desk. I sat and waited for what could not have been more than a minute, but time seemed to stretch. He then seemed to make a decision, then finally looked up at me.

"Stand up."

He looked me up and down and with a smile that only touched one side of his mouth he said,

"Well, at least you have a frame we can build on."

(I was very skinny as a child and had often heard the expressions,

"Av seen mer meet on a butchers pencil."

"Be careful crossing the road, you might fall down a drain".)

"You haven't done very well in the second test today, but because you did so well in the first test a few weeks ago, I am going to put today down to nerves and add both tests together. This will give you a good enough score to get into The Royal Corps of Signals."

Many years later, my brother told me that the Sergeant at the recruitment office was his friend and they

The Army

had conspired to make sure I would get into the army, which explained why he had changed my incorrect answers and the behaviour of the other Sergeant with his half smile.

On the sixth of May 1981, aged sixteen and a wee bit, I joined the Royal Corps of Signals. In the same intake, were 56 young men between 16 and 17 years old. About 10 were Scots, three or four where Welsh, and three where Irish. By chance, seven of the Scots ended up in the same room with one Welshman.

Basic training would consist of thirty-five weeks training spread over a year and a half, and a hell of a lot of running. Our main troop Sergeants where called Taff Tudgay and Sergeant Eddie (Dinger) Bell. Sergeant Tudgay seemed to treat everyone as the sons he never had and Eddie seemed to revel in the awe he caused by never seeming to miss anything that was going on. His favourite saying was "Go", as he pointed to something in the distance, to which everyone had to run, and if we were not quick enough we had to do it again.

I started to make friends, but like everyone else, I was either busy or tired, as both the days, evenings and sometimes nights where full. My fitness slowly increased and muscles started to form on what the Sergeant in Glasgow had referred to as my "frame".

About two weeks before I was due to finish my basic training, my troop Sergeant surprised me with some information. The troop was lined up outside the training wings waiting to march back to our accommodation, Sergeant Tudgay came up to me and handed me a piece of paper "carry this."

Why?

Then he shouted, "By the right, quick march".

When we arrived at the accommodation, we were dismissed.

"Hempsey", shouted Sergeant Tudgay.

"Yes Sergeant", I said as I moved towards him. He put out his hand for the paper I had been carrying.

"Did you read it?"

"No Sergeant."

"It's a report about you."

He looked at me as if waiting for a response, but all he could see was a face that had no expression, as my mind had gone completely blank. With no response, he continued.

"Your grades are not very good, you should be back trooped"

My stomach felt as if it just had a lead weight dropped into it, my mind remained empty. At a loss as to what to say or do, I just stared at him, motionless.

"But I have spoken to those above me on your behalf and persuaded them that you should not have to do the extra seven weeks training."

"No one from this intake will be back trooped."

"Thank you", was all I managed to say.

I don't know how those words managed to get uttered. I had just been condemned and reprieved in just under a minute. Two weeks later, our troop passed out of basic training with a large parade.

I then moved on to trade training, doing seven weeks of testing, repairing and faultfinding on telephone cables, and basic telephone repair. At the end of the course I had to sit several tests. On the last day the

The Army

instructors had everyone in one class and started to call out our names, giving each person their grades, then telling them which regiment they were being posted to. Then they got to me, "Hempsey."

"Yes, Sergeant."

"E pass," he announced.

"You're going to Third Armoured Division in Soest, Germany."

"On the hardest part of this course you managed an A, so if you want, we are prepared to allow you to stay on and redo the entire course, so that you can get the grade that we think you are capable of."

I was horrified at the thought that I might have to do it all again.

"No, thanks", rushed from my mouth.

Probably one of the quickest decisions I ever made.

Afterwards I couldn't believe what I had been offered or what I had accomplished.

The night before the hardest test, one of the lads on the course had suggested that we study together, so we spent several hours bouncing off each other. It was the first time I had ever studied with another person and to my surprise and some confusion, I managed an A Pass, something I had never before managed to do on any other test.

I would spend another week learning to maintain military vehicles and two weeks driver training, then three weeks leave before Germany.

To celebrate, I went for a few drinks with some friends; Dave"cookie"Cook, Knoxy and Johno. The NAAF's bar was almost full, but we saw a few seats

Why?

with some of the lads from basic training. Some I knew, some I did not.

We had not been sitting more than a few minutes when a Welsh lad that I had never had spoken to said very loudly.

"You're a Combat Lineman? That means your f—-ing thick."

There were about eight people around the table, which suddenly went very quite. I did not know what to say.

"I said, your f—-ing thick, stupid!"

I tried to ignore him.

"Hey, you thick jock."

I looked around the table as he continued his abuse. Still no one spoke, but they were all staring at me. I knew they expected me to say something, do something.

Shame and anger coursed through me, a part of me really wanted to rip his head off, but I was unable to. I just sat there looking at him, my face showing nothing.

Being a victim and suppressing my feelings had become so ingrained that I couldn't defend myself. I was conditioned by my past to just stand and take abuse, helpless and unable to show how I really felt.

The bar was full and noisy, but all I could hear was the total silence around the table, to my very core I felt ashamed, but even that I would not show. I could tell that everyone was embarrassed by my seeming cowardliness, as no one would look me in the eye, the Welsh man seemed to be satisfied with what he had done and walked off leaving me with my silence, I did what I had always done and tried to carry on as if nothing had

The Army

happened. This had always been possible as a child, but that child was gone and this had happened in front of my friends. They had just seen a new part of me, a part that I hated.

My shame was so great that after that night I never spoke to or tried to contact Dave, Knoxy or Johno again. In a few days I would go on leave before heading off to Germany, where no one would know me and where in just over a year, I would learn to express my anger.

I arrived in Germany on the 28th of June 1982, one month before my 18th birthday. The squadron was on manoeuvers when I got there, so my first few days were quiet. When they returned, everyone went straight to the bar, and it was there that I made my first mistake. I was asked what I wanted to drink.

Up to this point in my life, I had had only a couple of drinks, so I replied that I didn't really drink. You could have heard a pin drop. I knew that the people in my trade were renowned for working hard and drinking harder, and they were not about to let the tradition stop at me. I was politely threatened to start drinking or else.

By the time I was 18, I was in the bar every night learning to drink. It was probably the first thing that I thought I could do really well, and I managed to excel at it.

As a new guy in the squadron, one of the first jobs I was given was on the Regimental Police (RP) staff. This assignment often lasted three to six months, ending when the next new man came along. It was about the most hated job in the regiment, because it required you to do guard duty five days a week.

Why?

The camp had three places that had to be manned. One was on the main gate, doing one hour on and two hours off. The off times were spent escorting prisoners around. During all this, we had to wear full barrack dress — peaked hat, a two inch wide white plastic belt, trousers and very shiny boots.

The second was Sanger Guard, where we spent one hour on, one hour off, wore combat dress, and carried a rifle loaded with 10 live rounds, together with a little card that explained when you could or could not shoot someone.

The third was the HQ Guard Room, where we stood in a little box with a window, from eight in the morning till six in the evening, with just short breaks for lunch or to go to the toilet. All you did all day was salute officers. You were not allowed anything to help time pass; understandably no one wanted to do that job.

The man in charge of the guardroom and me was called Sergeant Ferry. There were a few other names he was known by, none of which were very flattering.

It didn't take me long before I started to dislike him. I understand now, that in my subconscious he had become my father and Benny – an incompetent man (which he probably wasn't), in a position of authority over me. And I had to rebel against him.

He would often discipline everyone for one man's mistake and like my father, for what was usually the most trivial of matters. Something that was expected in a training unit, but not in a working unit.

All that was needed was a complaint to get back to him that some Officer had not been saluted and he

The Army

would discipline everyone. Other days he just seemed to get out of the wrong side of the bed.

As the weeks passed, my hatred for him intensified to such an extent that when I was on Sanger Guard, I would often imagine shooting him, playing out in my mind the whole scenario. Lifting the rifle, pointing it and pulling the trigger; watching him die. Then the consequences of my action – he had a young child. I knew what it was like to grow up without a father, how could I do that to a child? So many times I imagined cocking the rifle and shooting him, but each time, the thought of his baby came into my thoughts, fortunately for me and him, my anger never found a route to fulfilment.

Things started to come to a head when two of the prisoners talked to each other about the charges against them. One of them was going through a court martial, so the other one told the Regimental Sergeant Major (RSM) what had been said, thus becoming a witness.

The RSM was not a happy man, so he gave the Provost Sergeant a hard time. Instead of trying to find out what had actually happened, the Provost Sergeant decided to take it out on his staff, even though the incident had happened out of our working hours. He ordered the four of us that were between duties outside to be lined up for a very public humiliation.

A few moments after we had lined up, he came out shouting, "MARK TIME" (To march on the spot).

I was standing the furthest from him, so at first he could not see that I was only just lifting my feet off the ground.

Why?

"LIFT YOUR BLOODY LEGS HEMPSEY." Unfortunately, in the army its illegal to disobey a direct order, but there was one way round it. During the time that I was supposed to be marking time — lifting each leg so that the knee was at a 45-degree angle to the body — I was only just getting my foot off the ground. It only took a few seconds before he was standing to the left of me, his face just a few inches from mine.

"LIFT YOUR BLOODY FEET HIGHER HEMPSEY", he shouted.

At first, anger coursed through my body, then a strange peace. I stared straight ahead at nothing, I could see him out of the corner of my eye, wearing his peek hat, pace-stick under his arm and his face red with anger.

"I SAID LIFT YOUR BLOODY LEGS HEMPSEY."

I continued to stare straight ahead, impassively ignoring his ranting.

"HALT", he shouted at every one.

" TO YOUR DUTIES, DISMISSED."

"HEMPSEY, GET INTO THE PRISONERS CELL."

I had been in the cell a few minutes when the guardroom Corporal entered.

"ATTENTION", he shouted.

Then Sergeant Ferry entered, again he stood to one side of me and immediately started shouting.

"HOW DARE YOU."

He ranted on for a few minutes more as I stared at the wall behind him, my face showing nothing. He must have realised that I was going to continue impassively ignoring him; his anger seemed to run out of steam. Frustrated, he turned and left the prisoners cell.

"TO YOUR DUTIES, DISMISSED", shouted the Guardroom Corporal.

I found that from then on, I pulled the HQ compound guard every day, in a little box about 10 foot by 6. All day, eight in the morning until six at night, effectively getting me out of the way.

At the end of the following week, the camp went on a higher state of alert, which meant all guard personnel would have to wear combat uniform. As it had happened overnight, I turned up for work in normal barrack dress. On arrival, I was told to go and change. I had arrived that morning as I had always done, twenty minutes early, but by the time I had returned it was just after eight. Sergeant Ferry immediately put me on a 'charge' for being late for work.

Within twenty minutes, he was marching me into my Squadron Commander's office like a puppet.

Sergeant Ferry read out the charge.

"Signalman Hempsey has been charged for being late for work."

That was all that was needed.

"Signalman Hempsey, I take a lack of discipline seriously."

"You're fined twenty pounds."

That was more than I earned in a day.

"Sargent, take him away."

Sergeant Ferry then marched a very angry eighteen year old back to work and into my little 10 by 6 box. I had now spent every day of the last week alone in the

Why?

small guard box wallowing in my anger. So much time to think about what had been going on; what had happened that morning was the last straw. I had had enough of the army and the only thing I could see to do was to go AWAL (Absent Without Authorised Leave).

It was Friday and the end of the month. The banks would be closed over the weekend and I had not made a request to go to the bank, so I would have to wait until Monday. My plan was simple – get some money, finish my shift then go. That would give me until the following morning to get as far away as possible. Unfortunately, my plan clashed with the Provost Sergeant.

On Monday morning, I went to work as normal. I was nervous, but also relieved I had made a decision to go and nothing was going to change that. I only needed to get to the bank to finance my little trip. The Provost Corporal was in the guardroom early.

"Good morning Corporal", I said.

"Hi Joe."

"Ah, could I be relieved today to get to the bank."

"Yea, I'll arrange it for you."

"Cheers Corporal."

And off I went to the little box to salute officers for the rest of the day. My lunchtime relief came just after noon. I asked if he knew anything about me being relieved later for the bank.

"Sorry Joe I don't know anything, I've just been told that you have to come straight back here when you've finished lunch and not to the main guard room."

At 2 o'clock I rang the main guardroom.

"Provost Corporal."

The Army

"It's Hempsey, I was wondering when someone was coming to relieve me?"

"Don't worry Hempsey, someone will be up shortly."

Then he hung up. By 2.30 I was getting worried. The bank would be closed at 3.30, so I called again and got the same answer. The same thing happened on Tuesday and Wednesday.

I shared a room with three others, only one of which I trusted, Ian Rigby. I had told him what I planned, which he thought was great. That week he was the communications driver. At any time, a secure communication could be received and a driver would take a copy to several different army camps. The messages could come in day or night, so he suggested that if he got called out at night he would drop me off in town. Wednesday night he got a call at around 11 o'clock. I quickly packed a bag and as we left camp, I hid in the back of the land rover.

"I am going to drop this stuff off first. It'll take a few hours, you might as well get some sleep in the back."

"Yeah, no problem."

I had learnt a long time ago to sleep anywhere, so I got as comfortable as possible in the back of the land rover.

When I woke up the land rover had come to a stop. Out of the back of the vehicle I could see daylight. I sat up and went numb with incomprehension, I was back at camp and Ian stuck his head in the back.

"Sorry Joe, I didn't have the time to drop you off."

"I don't believe you Ian."

Why?

"I didn't Joe, I'm sorry."

It took me a few moments to express to him how I felt, to which he still replied with a small shrug of his shoulders.

"I'm sorry Joe."

I had to quickly accept the reality that I had to go to work again.

Thursday was the same, I was told in the morning that someone would be sent to relieve me, but it never happened. All this was adding to my frustration and making me more determined to go AWAL. On Friday it started all over again, each time I phoned the guardroom I was told,

"Don't worry, someone will be right up to relieve you."

At 2.30 on Friday afternoon, one of the lads was sent up. I had one hour to get into town before the banks closed for the weekend. It took two minutes to walk from the HQ compound to the main guardroom. Normally, a driver would be waiting for anyone that needed to get to the bank. There were about eight people in the guardroom when I got there, some immediately left the room, the others would not even look at me. A little confused I said,

"Corporal, who will be taking me to the bank?"

"No, you will have to arrange your own transport." Said the Guardroom Corporal.

"But, it's always arranged."

"Well, you shouldn't have pissed off Ferry."

This took me so close to breaking. My whole body felt as if it was about to explode with uncontrolled emotions, it took all my will power not to break down. Even talking became difficult. My body seemed to want to betray how much I felt that I had been beaten.

I stood silently for about ten minutes at the back of the guardroom, aware that everyone was going out of their way not to be around me.

The only solution I had left was to go to the squadron lines and see if someone there would give me a lift.

I moved towards the guardroom door.

"Where do you think you're going to Hempsey?" said the Corporal.

"To my squadron lines."

It was a struggle to get the words out and fortunately there was no reply, so I kept walking.

Two squadron shared an old star-shaped prison; the prisoner's cells were used as storage for the different trades. It was always busy, but today it was deserted. Walking down the empty corridors seemed as unreal as how I felt. At the end of my squadron's corridor I could see someone's silhouette against an open door. As I approached, I realised that it was my Squadron Sergeant Major. He was looking onto the vehicle park, watching as all the men were making the final preparations for manoeuvres (pretending to be at war), that were due to start on Monday morning.

"Excuse me Sir."

He turned towards me.

"Yes Hempsey?"

I tried to explain what had been going on, but the emotions behind how I felt had become too great, tears

Why?

welled in my eyes. Every word I spoke was strained with emotions.

He looked down or into the compound, but not at me.

"GO AWAY", he said harshly.

I stopped for a moment before realising he was pointing his pace stick at someone that was approaching us.

"Go on Hempsey", he said.

I finished a few moments later.

"Don't worry, I will sort this out with the guard room, just wait here and I will arrange for you to get to the bank."

True to his word, within a few minutes I was on my to the way to the bank, just getting there before it closed at Three Thirty. I now had the money, but I could not just walk out the front gates with a large bag and wait for a taxi, just two days before the whole regiment was due to go on manoeuvres. That might cause someone in the guardroom to ask me some difficult questions.

That night I tried to arrange a lift into town with the help of my room mate Ian, it ended up being a little bit more difficult than I thought. Everyone from my squadron had been ruled out, simply because I did not really know any of them. Would they give me a lift to the train station or the guardroom? I didn't know and wasn't prepared to find out. Ian also spent the night trying to persuade me not to go. A part of me wanted to listen to his very good reasons to not go, most notably that I would eventually have to go to jail. My thoughts and emotions swung between how much trouble I

The Army

would be in if I went AWAL, to a deeper feeling of dread if I had to go back on guard duty. Ian persuaded me to at least leave it till Saturday morning, have a few drinks and sleep on it.

Saturday morning came and I knew there was no way I could carry on; I had to leave.

Ian went off into the other squadron accommodation, looking for someone he knew with a car. A short time later he returned with a big smile.

"Joe I've got you a lift, one of the lads from two Squadron will take you to the train station in about twenty minutes."

"I hope this one's not going to bring me back!" I said with a touch of sarcasm and a small smile.

"NO, no, no, he's fine, but there's one problem! He's a Corporal."

"Shit Ian, did you tell him."

"No."

"Ok, let's get my bags out of here Ian, before too many people wake."

As we were going into town I was very quiet, not really wanting to get into conversation, in case he asked why I was going on leave two days before the regiment was going on manoeuvres. When I got my bags out of his car I offered him some money, which he refused, saying with the second big smile I had seen that morning,

"If you are going AWAL, then you are going to need all the money you have."

Fortunately for me, he found helping a junior rank go AWAL very amusing.

Why?

During the time I was AWAL, I received a share of the compensation that had been awarded to me following my father's death. I gave some of it to my sister, as when she had turned 18 she had given almost all of her money to our mother to buy some much needed things for the home.

However, this still left me with just over £4,000 in the bank. The first week I spent with my brother Mick, as I thought that if I went to my mother's home the police or the army would pick me up after seven days. I thought that I had better show my face to my mother. It was mid-week and just after 8p.m.when I entered the house. My mother already had her coat on, as she was just about to go out. We had a hug, then she apologized, saying that she had already made arrangements for the night and had to go straight away or she would be late.

I stood by the window talking to my sister Margaret, when I noticed out of the corner of my eye that my mother had stopped and was talking to someone. Glancing away from my sister, I took in the whole scene; two policemen and a man in army uniform had stopped my mother, who had just reached the gate, which was less than 30 seconds from the front door. They told her that her son had gone AWAL and asked her if she had seen him. At first she said no, thinking that they were talking about my younger brother Neil who was also in the army and whom she immediately thought was the one most likely to do something so stupid.

Then the coin dropped, they were referring to her other son, the quiet one she did not expect to do anything rash or stupid. A few minutes later, my mother

The Army

stormed back into the house, very angry, but not really knowing what to do with her wayward 18-year-old son. She quickly tried to persuade me to return, I just said no. I was still standing by the window as I watched the police get into three cars and drive away. I thought it better not to stay at my mothers, not just because the police wanted to have a word with me.

Just before I joined the army, I had started to hang around with Geoff Hamilton, who lived just along the street from me. He now had a friend called Choker (because he always had his right hand at his throat).

I started taking them out quite regularly for a drink. Both of them smoked, which I ribbed them about. Unfortunately, I should have been listening to what I was saying because within a month I was doing it as well.

I constantly felt some pressure about going back to the army; it became really obvious to me after a night in a disco. Several police officers entered, some in uniform and some in plain clothes. They walked around the edge of the dance floor looking for someone. So, with the help of the liquid bravery that I had been drinking, I started to make some sarcastic comments as one of them drew near.

Immediately Jeff and Choker stood between the Officers and me. They spoke alternately:

"What are you doing?"

"Are you stupid?"

"Do you want to get caught?"

I had no answer for them. I guess a part of me did want to be caught, so that the decision to return to Germany would be taken away from me.

Why?

I stayed away for 62 days in all, during which, I found an old saying to be very true: 'A fool and his money are soon parted.'

Eventually, I met another soldier by the name of Danny Robertson, who was on authorised leave from his unit in Germany. He would be returning to his unit in a few days. So, with only a little encouragement from mother, sister, brothers and friends, I decided to travel back with him, minus several thousand pounds. I am still not sure how or what it was spent or what it was spent on, but I had consumed a lot of alcohol and had a new addiction — cigarettes.

The night I got back to my camp the Guard Commander was not very happy with me turning up on his duty because of the extra paperwork it would cause. He suggested that I should come back the following day.

I was put on open arrest for about two weeks, and then I was sent back to normal duties. In all it took two months for me to be charged, during which time the army would not give me my full pay, just in case I decided to leave again. Each week I bought some cigarettes and a book. By the time the charge came to fruition I had found out how great it was to escape into books, and for several years there was not a time when I did not have a book by the side of my bed.

When I was eventually charged, I was sentenced to fifty days. I spent the first ten days in the regimental guardroom; fortunately the Provost Sergeant left me alone.

My feelings of anger towards him were gone, so it wasn't as bad as it could have been. After the first ten

The Army

days, I was escorted back to the UK to serve the rest of my sentence at the main army jail in Colchester. I spent a further twenty three days in Colchester, earning seventeen-days remission for good behaviour. I thought I had done quite well, thirty three days in military jail for a sixty two-day holiday.

I left Colchester super fit, but on returning to Germany I found it easier exercising my arm in the bar than my body in the gym. I no longer felt the need to go AWAL, as something in me had simply changed. My new escape at the age of 18 was books and alcohol; I no longer needed to physically run away. I would do it in other ways.

Not long after I returned to my unit, volunteers were requested from my squadron to form a boxing team. Out of the entire squadron only one man volunteered and it wasn't me.

When it became obvious that no one else was going to volunteer, the whole squadron was ordered to the gym, where we where lined up, shortest on the left tallest on the right. The PTIs (physical training instructors) moved us around until we were more evenly matched by weight than by height.

As I was slim, I was moved down a bit to the left, where I was matched more evenly with someone my own weight. When we where all evenly matched, one of the PTIs pointed at the largest two men.

"You and you fight."

There were quite a few fights before it worked its way down to me and the person that I would have to fight.

Why?

" You and you fight."

By now my adrenaline levels must have been very high as I went in swinging a fast I could.

The guy they put me with was a lot smaller and his reach was far shorter. After only 30 seconds we had to be stopped, my opponent was putting up no defence against my wildly swung punches.

We went back to standing against the wall and continued watching as everyone else took their turn. Right at the end, the PE instructor pointed to me again.

"You and you, fight."

The other person he pointed to was heavier and a bit taller than the last one.

Again we were stopped quickly, as I was just too quick with my arm for him to even throw a punch at me.

Again I returned to my place in the line and watched as others were being told to fight again. Again I was pointed at, "you and you fight."

The other man he pointed to was up at the bigger end of the line, he must have been a good 30 or 40 pounds heavier and more than four inches taller, a much bigger difference than the two I had already fought.

Adrenaline pumping and arms swinging, I went for him. All of a sudden he was more than 10 feet away from me, and everything had a reddish, pink colour.

He was coming at me again but strangely with his hand down. I still had my hands up by my face and started towards him. My hearing seemed to return from a distance, "Stop, Stop, Stop!"

The Army

The larger guy had hit me square on the nose, causing me to stagger back, blood was pouring from my face. One of the troop Sergeants said,

"Hempsey, go get yourself cleaned up", pointing towards the toilets.

Shaken, I walked to the toilets and tried to clean away some of the blood; my eyesight had not returned properly, but I could see that that my nose was broken.

As my vision wasn't returning to normal, I was sent to the medical centre.

The medic's diagnosis was very quick.

"You're OK, and a broken nose will give your face more character."

This event had a bit of a Pandora's Box effect on me; it showed me for the first time that I could fight back instead of being the victim, feeling that everyone was too big for me.

I had years of pent up anger and this marked the beginning of a violent time for me. I was drinking heavily, which removed some more of my inhibitions leaving me free to lash out at others more easily. Fortunately, the army was a good place to be able to vent anger, as no one ever let a fight get out of hand, breaking it up quickly. So no real damage was ever really done, although I have forgotten how many more times I broke my nose and once managed to fracture my jaw and wrist.

Acting out my anger only caused me to become even more disenchanted with life. One night after I had returned to the camp from another night out drinking, I felt immensely lonely. I understand now that I had a very poor self-image and even worse social skills. Al-

Why?

though I was almost always surrounded by people, I often felt immensely lonely.

I found conversations very difficult, as I had spent so much of my childhood not talking, so forming relationships was almost impossible.

That night as I sat drunk on the edge of my bed, I looked at my life and could not remember a single time from my childhood when I was happy. There were only painful memories and so much of it was missing. My education was so poor that I thought it impossible to make anything more of my life; my past seemed to be a black, empty thing.

When I looked at what the future might hold, all I could see was more blackness and pain. I felt I just couldn't take it anymore. There was just no point in going on, nothing worth living for. I had had several illnesses over the years, so I had quite a collection of pills that I had not bothered to take, so I got them all out and took them, washing them down with some straight vodka. I had finally given up on life.

As I was taking them, I felt very calm about what I was doing; then I lay down and went straight to sleep.

To my great surprise, I woke up the next morning.

It was a Sunday, so I had no work. I managed to stagger to the toilet, bumping off the walls on either side of the corridor on the way. I looked in the mirror, my pupils were completely dilated and I just felt like death warmed up, I staggered back to my bed.

If anyone did see me, I am sure they would have just put it down to a Sunday morning hangover; very common in the single men's accommodation.

The Army

As I lay in bed, I noticed a small black spider under the skin of my left hand. Whether I was hallucinating or not I don't know, but for the next several hours I lay on my bed chasing this little spider with a pin trying to dig it out until eventually it disappeared.

I don't remember much more of that day. I did manage some food, but I was in and out of sleep most of the time and my mind was not quite with it.

I have always thought of that night's sleep as being a 'dead sleep'; emptier than any other I'd ever had.

From that night on I never spiraled down to such a deep depression, and part of me felt that I could not even commit suicide properly, although over the next few years I would often consider it.

The following morning I was back at work as normal. That particular Monday there was an inspection by my Squadron Sergeant Major and the Commanding Officer of the squadron. I still had what was left of the bottle of vodka by the side of my bed. I remember looking at it and thinking I must put it away, as it is a chargeable offence to have alcohol in the single men's accommodation, but I forgot all about it.

At 10 o'clock, as I was going for my morning tea-break and was passing Squadron Admin offices, the Squadron Sergeant Major just happened to be passing at the same moment and unexpectedly turned to me and said. "Hempsey, get into my office, NOW!"

It was obvious he was pissed at me, but for what? Although I had been drunk a lot recently, there was nothing I could think of that would warrant me being disciplined.

Why?

As I stood outside his office I was racking my brain, what could I have possibly done that he would know about? But I could think of nothing.

The Squadron Sergeant Major passed me to enter his office, looking like a bull that has just eaten something nasty. Then from his office he shouted,

"Get in here!"

I thought this was a good time to put some of my army training into practice, so I came to attention lifting my right leg until it was 45 degrees from the ground, then slammed it down so it made an impressive sound, then marched into his office where I halted in front of his desk.

"Do you know why you're here Hempsey?"

"No Sir."

"Are you sure?"

Just then an image of the half-consumed bottle of vodka sitting beside my bed flashed in front of my eyes.

"No, Sir", really hoping it wasn't the alcohol.

"Maybe this will jog your memory," he said, lifting the bottle of vodka onto his desk.

There was something comical about the whole thing, so I just wanted to laugh, but this wasn't the place for that. Taking a deep breath and holding it, I tried not to laugh out loud, but no matter how hard I tried I couldn't stop smiling. I was caught between the need to be serious and the need to fall over laughing, and I was going bright red as the air started forcing its way out of my lungs making strange choking sounds.

The Army

Fortunately, the Squadron Sergeant Major started doing the same thing, but still he had to discipline me and not laugh at the same time.

"Hempsey, this is a serious discipline problem."

By now he was having problems talking, which was only making me worse.

I couldn't take him seriously when he was obviously trying his hardest and failing not to smile. I took another deep breath and said slowly,

"Yesss, Sssirrr."

"You are a senior signalman in the squadron and should know better."

Again I had to take a deep breath.

"Yesss, Sssirrr."

"How many extra guard duties do you think this deserves?"

"Aaah, one, Sir", I said hopefully.

"ONE! NO, TAKE THREE!"

I knew I was getting off very lightly, so trying not to smile too much, I said,

" Thank you, Sir."

"Get out of here, Hempsey."

I came to attention and turned to my right, but before I could march away the SSM said,

"Consider yourself lucky Hempsey; that I don't drink vodka. Get a bag and get this out of my sight."

I never did the three guard extra duties.

My job gave me the money for my more destructive habits; drinking which I had become very good at, spending almost all of my monthly pay on it and fighting, which I was not good at.

Why?

The fighting virtually stopped after I came across an American. I was in a local British soldiers' bar called the Big Ben. It was the middle of the week, so there were not many people there. I noticed that the person beside me had an American accent, we got to talking and he told me that he was part Native American Indian, serving in Germany with the US Army. After a few minutes of talking I literally felt anger well up from deep inside and uncontrollably, I lashed out at him. A short scuffle ensued before we were pulled apart. He left the bar and I carried on drinking as normal. But something was different this time, I was confused as to why I had lashed out at him; he had done nothing to provoke my actions. That night, the alcohol numbed me from the feelings of guilt I would feel over the coming days and weeks, as I replayed that moment over and over again in my mind.

A few weeks later I met him again in the same bar. He came up to me and we started to chat, I apologised for what I had done and he was very gracious in accepting my apology, simply saying it was OK, but again, within a few minutes the anger welled up from within and I lashed out at him. The next few weeks I became increasingly troubled by the way I had been behaving towards him. I could not understand why I was being violent toward him, as both times he had done nothing to provoke me and had not even tried to fight back.

It was not long before I saw him in the bar, this time I approached him, as I needed off load my guilt by apologising for what I had done.

"Aah Hi."

He turned and looked me in the eye.

"Aah I'm sorry for what I done."
"It's alright ", he said.
"I don't even know why I've done it."

He shrugged his shoulders and we stood in silence for a few moments. Strangely, I felt very peaceful within, then I felt it, welling up from within like a wave. I just grabbed his shirt and hit him. Time seemed to stand still, then an unusual thought went through my mind,

"Go on then, hit me."

But he didn't, as he had not on the other occasions. Hands grabbed me and we were pulled apart, I fell to the floor and was pinned down by someone that was bleeding and it was dripping into my eyes. He was saying something, but the anger within me was gone, leaving me numb. He could have beaten me and I would not have cared.

Something in me changed after that moment. I stopped lashing out at others, and for many years I felt a terrible guilt for what I had done, and confused over that one simple thought,

"Go on then, hit me."

And why did I stop to let him hit me? Slowly over the next decade I started to understand some of what I had learnt that night.

Each time I got into a fight and was hit by the other person, a deeper part of me felt justified for what I had done. When the American did not hit back, it stopped me feeling justified; he had cut me off from a deeper part of my psyche that allowed me to feel justified when others fought back.

Why?

And for years I was troubled by the thought that maybe I wanted others to hurt me, as pain had become the only emotion I seemed to understand.

It must have taken me over ten years to stop feeling guilty. Then, as I slowly started to understand the changes he had caused, I started to mentally thank him for what he had done.

Each time I lashed out at him he forgave me. Maybe he could not express his anger, or maybe he was an example of non-violence and how over a period of time it changes people from within.

Unfortunately, it did not change my other destructive habit; drinking.

In 1985 my stay in Germany came to an end and I was posted to 30 Signal Regiment in Dorset. The nearest town, Blandford, was about two miles away. It was a nice, scenic little place in the middle of nowhere, which was its biggest problem, as I had become used to late night pubs and nightclubs in Germany, but this place didn't have a nightlife. All the pubs closed at 10.30 in the winter and 11 o'clock in the summer, and that was it.

A far cry from Germany where I could get a drink till five or six in the morning.

Fortunately, my stay in Blandford was broken up, firstly with a trip to Cyprus on a three-week exercise. This was great, as there were only six of us from the squadron. We ended up doing one day on and one day off, and the weekends off as well.

So I started to party, more than once getting in just before I was due to start work, which did not impress the Corporal in charge, who threatened to have me sent

The Army

back to the UK if I did not stop drinking, neither of which happened.

I also managed to get the worst sunburn of my life. After being there a week, all the other lads were getting a bit of a tan, so I went to a beach for several hours without any sunscreen, which for a Scotsman is not a good idea.

I only started to notice it on my way back to the camp as I could feel the sun beating on my legs. I ended up bright red down to my shorts, then bright white, then from the bottom of my shorts, bright red again.

Everywhere ended up blistering and at night, if I moved, the pain woke me, so I had to push myself off the bed, turn around and then gently lie back down again. I couldn't even go to see the army doctor for some cream, as I may have been charged with causing a self-inflicted wound.

I also started to walk like a cowboy who had been on a horse for too long, as the blisters at the top of my legs became open cuts. So it was no more shorts or short-sleeved shirts for me.

Just then someone decided to arrange a trip to Ayia Napa, which is renowned for its beautiful beaches. Not to be put off by a bit of severe sunburn, I went along in jeans and a long sleeved shirt. As I walked onto the beach, I took one look at the crowd's limited beachwear, and then at myself, I felt like a total nerd.

As much as I wanted to enjoy the beautiful beach and scenery, I couldn't in my over-dressed state. Fortunately, there was a bar nearby (but not on the beach) in

Why?

which I managed to forget my sunburn and my sorrow as the lads had a good time on the beach.

After three weeks we were heading back to the UK on an RAF Hercules. As I entered it I was given a lunch box and a set of ear defenders for the noise. The seating was basic webbing, with my back to the windows facing into the centre of the plane.

Just before take off, the captain came out and told us the duration of the flight, our altitude and as a parting comment said,

"Don't worry if you see some of the flight crew panic during the flight, its normal on these old planes like."

It was an eight-hour flight. I could not speak to the person beside me because of the noise of the engines. About half way through the flight two of the crew came out and started to have what looked like a heated conversation with very worried looks on their faces. The conversation lasted long enough for everyone to notice them, and then they rushed to the windows overlooking the wings and stared intently out of the airplane.

By now everyone was trying to figure out why the crew was looking so worried; turning around to try and see what they where looking at. After a few minutes, they turned around and met in the centre of the airplane and had another heated conversation. With exaggerated shrugs and looks of relief they walked back to the cockpit leaving behind some very pissed off people who were beginning to realise that this was the crew's way of breaking the boredom of a long flight – just frighten your passengers a little bit. As I looked around, I noticed that for a group of people that had just come from a

The Army

sunny climate, an awful lot of them looked extremely white.

On returning to my unit, I was told that as far as any other trips away were concerned, my name was at the bottom of the list (not because of my drinking though). Two weeks later a trip to Belize in Central America came up. I immediately volunteered to go and almost as quickly was told, "No, you've just returned from Cyprus". There were about 12 other men who would be before me and for some madness; all of them refused the trip because it started in the middle of the squadron's three-week block leave. All of them said they had made other arrangements.

I was amazed that none of them wanted to go, as it would mean four months in the Caribbean and an entitlement to four weeks' leave on your return.

So two weeks later, on the 6th of August 1985, I went to Central America armed with lots of factor 20 sunscreen. During my time there I had to learn to fix and repair far more complicated equipment than I had been trained for. This job was usually done by tele-mechs and was a far cry from what I had been trained for, although I knew the basics. So they threw me in at the deep end and I learnt very quickly, managing to pick up more in four months than I did in three years in Germany.

Belize also happens to have a great climate and some coral reefs, which on one occasion I was lucky enough to swim in and explore. They have an amazing variety of colours and shapes that are constantly changing; I stayed in the water for six hours, only getting out at the

Why?

end of the day. It was one of the most beautiful experiences I've ever had.

I had been in the army for almost six years now and in my trade I should have been promoted to Lance Corporal in just over three years, so I was way behind. I was not really aware of it then, but I was afraid of the responsibility and that I would in some way, be found lacking.

I wanted the promotion, but at the same time was afraid of it. I had still managed to hide my lack of education, and to get a promotion I would have to start going on courses. That started to scare me, so I started to feel trapped. The prospect of leaving the army to go into an uncertain world left me cold and the very real fear that people would find out what I was really like also made me feel afraid, there seemed nothing that I could do and nothing that I wanted to do, so doing nothing was safe.

I really felt that I needed some sort of guidance; anything, so out of desperation I started reading horoscopes from daily newspapers. Almost every day they would state that change was just around the corner, but each day was the same as the last; so I was just plodding along with life as I had always done, afraid to make any decision, but for the first time since joining the army I felt that something had to change.

Fortunately, circumstances were about to force me into making the change I desperately wanted, but was so afraid to make.

I had been back from Belize for about eight months when I was told I had to go on an upgrading course in

The Army

another camp to get my Class 1 Combat Lineman Certificate. Even with that, I got a helping hand from the Corporal in charge of the entrance test, as I had still managed to fail it.

The journey to the training camp would be by an overnight train, arriving early the following morning. It was about seven when I walked into the camp, carrying three bags; one over my back and one in each hand. The road was wide enough for four vehicles and was divided by a central reservation that had some small trees. As I was walking to where my new accommodation would be, I noticed an officer on the pavement at the far side of the carriageway.

As my hands were full and I was tired, and not in uniform, I decided he was just too far away to have to shout,

"Good morning, Sir."

But a few minutes after I had passed him, I heard a pair of steel-shod boots running and someone shouting. It was the camp Provost Sergeant; he was a bit red in the face as he came up to me and demanded to know why I had not said good morning to the officer. I thought I had better plead ignorance and say,

"Sorry Sergeant, I did not notice him."

After telling me that I should be more aware, he took my name and squadron, and ranted on in a loud voice about discipline for a couple of minutes. I did what everyone in the army does; I let it wash over me, in one ear and out the other; a standard practice in the army when confronted with someone in a bad mood. When

Why?

he had finished, I went to my new squadron lines as if nothing had happened.

I was just getting settled in when a Lance Corporal came up to the room asking for me. He told me that I was in deep trouble (but not as politely as that) and that I was wanted in the troop office immediately. When I got there, the Troop Sergeant proceeded to give me a hard time. When he was finished, he sent me to the Troop Staff Sergeant who did virtually the same thing. He then passed me on to the Troop Officer, a one-pip wonder just out of training and younger than me, who also proceeded to give me a hard time.

After he was finished, he sent me on to the Squadron Sergeant Major. By now things were no longer going in one ear then out the other, the SSM not only gave me a hard time, but 10 extra guard duties. In one month I would normally have to do two or three guard duties, but now over the next month I would have to do 12 or 13; one night on, one night off and still have to do my normal duties during the day.

I was not a happy person at all.

At 5.30 p.m. that night, the whole squadron was called on parade; several hundred men from different courses. We were told that there was a thief in the accommodation, so until he owned up (as if he would), everyone would be confined to the accommodation block and put on a 'Bull Night' until further notice. If the army had its own dictionary, Bull Night would come under the same sort of heading as Bull s—-. We would all have to clean the accommodation block to a very high standard, from polishing the floors to scrubbing

The Army

the toilets. Normally these would all be done on a daily basis, but a Bull Night would mean hours of cleaning. Some of the lads on my course went to the Troop offices to try and explain that it could not possibly have been anyone from our course that was the thief, as we had only arrived that morning, but no one in the office seemed to be able to grasp that simple concept, so we would be doing the Bull Night with everyone else. The most stupid part of it was that we would have to make bed blocks. This was done with our sheets and blankets, folding them so that they made a square that would sit at the head of the bed, with the pillows on top, a total pain, as none of us had done anything like that since basic training several years ago.

Again, the next morning the squadron was put on parade in front of the accommodation block.

One of the Sergeants shouted.

"Squadron Attention", followed by a loud bang, as several hundred boots slammed into the ground. The Staff Sergeant that had put us on the Bull Night stepped forward with his pace stick held firmly under his arm.

"I take theft very seriously and the cowardly thief that is amongst yous still has not owned up, therefore I have no other choice than to continue with Bull Nights indefinitely until he does."

"This is your last chance to own up."

I just thought, "I've had enough of this shit".

He left a silence for a few moments as he waited on someone owning up. Of course no one did.

"To your duties, dismissed", someone shouted.

Why?

The frustration of everything that had been going on made me make a snap decision; I would have to get to the Staff Sergeant before he disappeared. I tried to push through the crowd of soldiers that were trying to get back into the accommodation, constantly trying to keep the Staff Sergeant in sight, but with so many people trying to get back into the accommodation, it was difficult. He disappeared then reappeared several times. I moved as quickly as possible; finally I caught sight of him standing by the doors letting the crowd pass.

"Excuse me, Staff.

He turned to me

"What?!"

"I want to PVR" (Personal Voluntary Release). Basically, it meant that I wanted to buy myself out of the army.

I saw a moment of surprise, which he quickly shrugged off saying, "See me later".

He quickly turned away, stepping into the crowd and was gone. It was obviously not a conversation he wanted to get into.

I had had enough, but I still had to go to work. I went with the lads to the first morning of trade training. The instructor there started by saying that,

"If anyone does not wish to be on this course, they should put their hand up now and I will have them sent back to their working unit."

So I put my hand up, much to his surprise. Apparently I had been the only person who had ever done it.

He ordered me out of the class and asked why. I explained what had happened and he said,

The Army

"Don't worry, I will sort it out."

"It's too late for that", was my reply.

I was out of the army two months later and they still owe me some money. On reflection, fate pushed me to make a decision that I was not otherwise prepared to make, as the army had become a safe place to hide.

I knew I had been extremely fortunate with the army, as it allowed me to do many things that I would not normally have done. AB-sailing, canoeing, mountain climbing, skiing and digging holes in the middle of winter or standing outside in sub zero temperatures doing guard duty, as well as many other similarly unforgettable things.

Why?

Chapter Three

Another New Beginning

On the Fourteenth of December 1987, I walked out of an army camp for the last time after six years, two hundred and seventy two days. Not that I was counting, as two weeks before, I was given my release documents/references with the exact length of time I had spent in the army. The first bit impressed me, then I read the bit about conduct. There were four categories ranging from 'Outstanding' down to 'Unsatisfactory'. I was rated 4th out of the five categories, it might as well have said, "Trouble maker, don't bother employing". I appealed to my commanding officer, but was told that it could not be changed because I had gone AWAL almost five years before.

I had joined the army at sixteen and now I was twenty three, leaving with two bags of clothes and nowhere to live. I thought I was entitled to help with resettlement, as I had been in the army for more than five years, but again I was told that the time spent training under the age of eighteen did not count towards time spent in the army as an adult. I would be given no help in rejoining civilian life, which like many service men, I was not prepared for.

Another New Beginning

The events over the next four years would be particularly stressful and parts of it I would look back on years later and doubt my own sanity. I have written it as I remember it happening, but I am not sure if parts of it only took place in my mind. Stress, depression, alcohol and loneliness would define this period of my life.

My brother Liam picked me up from the camp and arranged for me to sleep on the couch of his friend's home in Southampton for a few days until I found somewhere to live. I was overdrawn at the bank, as it had cost me several hundred pounds to buy myself out of the army. I had applied for a few, but nothing had come of them, so I had no choice but to find the cheapest place possible to live in. Within two days I was moving into a single room, which would cost twenty two pounds a week, with no cooking facilities.

The room was so small that I could stand with one arm over the bed touching a wall with my fingertips, and as I stretched out my other arm, I was less than two centimetres away from touching the other wall.

It was a very large, old Victorian house and I think my room was once an airing cupboard.

I purchased a small microwave oven and lived off packaged food, so I soon started to lose weight.

With the help of my brothers I got a few days here and there working as a labourer. Disillusionment soon started to settle in. I was spending most days alone often just wandering about with no real purpose, hardly speaking to anyone for days, but I kept hoping that there was something better coming for me than this constant struggle and almost endless emptiness.

Why?

On one of my long walks, I came across a Tarot reader who worked from a little corner in a restaurant. I hadn't the money for a reading, but I thought that when I did, I would visit her; maybe she would have some answers.

Several weeks later I had enough money for a reading, so I went to see the tarot reader.

"Can I have a reading?"

"Yes", she replied, as she offered me a seat opposite her.

"Have you ever had a reading before?"

"No", I admitted, trying to put on as bland a face as possible, so that she would not read how I was really feeling. She then passed me a pack of cards, saying, "Please shuffle these".

I shuffled and passed them back to her and she laid some of them out on the table. She supposedly proceeded to look into my future.

She said nothing that sticks in my memory, but then she started to talk about life after death and said that her beliefs could prove that there was a reason to life; that life was not about the constant struggle just to make ends meet.

This was in some way what I had been looking for, something that could prove that there was a meaning to my life. I was so relieved to have found something that might prove that there was a reason to life, that I broke down and cried.

Maybe this was what I had been looking for since my early childhood when I had often thought, "There must be more to life than this".

Another New Beginning

She told me where some Spiritualist Churches were and that they could help me to develop psychic skills so that I could prove to myself that there was life after death and that God did exist.

Something she said also caused me to phone my mother and for probably the first time, tell her that I loved her and that it had taken a long time for me to understand how much she had sacrificed in bringing up five children. We both shed some tears for a time.

Around the same time as all this was going on, I had a very vivid dream of my brother Liam, in which he died. Because it was so vivid I tried searching for a deeper meaning, hoping that it was not some sort of premonition. I did manage to find a dream analysis book that seemed to explain it, saying that the person who died would in some way be responsible for a change in the dreamer's life!

The first Spiritualist Church I went to invited me into what was called an 'open circle', to try to develop psychic skills. It started with a small prayer, then I was told to meditate and allow any mental pictures to form.

Nearing the end of the meditation, one of the two ladies running the circle stood up to do what I was later told was trance mediumship.

The curtains were closed and the lights off, yet the lighting in the room was still quite good, as it was an early summer's evening.

I was surprised to see quite clearly what looked like another younger woman standing partly inside the lady who had stood up. I blinked several times, but it did not go away. The lady then started to talk, but I was

Why?

not really listening, as I was focused on what I was seeing, catching only bites of what was being said. If this ghost was to be believed, the world was about to be destroyed, but as a consolation we would be ok. As she sat down I could no longer see anything behind her.

But my biggest surprise was when the other, supposedly more experienced medium who was running the group said to her, "Thank you, that was such a softly spoken *young man*".

And to add to my confusion, the lady that had done the Trance mediumship replied, "Yes he was".

Since I had witnessed something that I could not explain, even though it contradicted the more experienced people who where running the circle, I clung to the hope that there was something in all this. Even if, according to the medium's guide, the world was about to fall apart at any time. I never went back to that particular psychic circle and I was to find in the future, time after time, that psychic groups where run by people that did not really know what they where doing.

I started to spend a lot of money on Tarot readers, always being told that things would be better next month, next year; always something in the future, never now.

I found myself not really living in the now, never finding happiness in this moment, so I was always hoping that the future held something better.

Things were not going well with my landlord, as I had been out of work and claiming unemployment benefit, so he had to wait for the state to send him the rent. He started making my life awkward, then he tried to evict me. When it got to court, his case was thrown out and I was awarded costs, as he had been trying to evict me illegally. Fortunately, not long after, Liam and Neil bought a house, so I became a lodger with them.

I found that as an ex-serviceman I was entitled to go on a free government training course without having to be unemployed for six months, as is normal for most people. I applied, hoping that I would be able to get a placement with a company doing the same work I was trained for in the army.

The first week of the course was in a classroom doing written tests, then they would find a placement for me with a company. At the beginning of the second week I was told what they thought I was capable of doing and to my surprise they offered me a placement to train me as an assistant manager for a large chain of convenience stores. It just seemed too alien for me to go from the army to working in a shop. I had never considered myself the type of person who could work in a shop, never mind being its manager, so I turned it down telling them again that I had hoped they could get me a placement working in some sort of telecoms company.

They told me that they would try, and if a placement came up in the area I wanted, they would get in touch. The next month was more difficult than normal. At least when I was busy looking for a job it gave me something to do, but now I was relying on the course to do it for me, which left me with nothing to do at all but wait, wait, wait; which I found very difficult.

Why?

After a month, I received a letter saying that they had found a placement for me. I was excited and a bit nervous as I went along to this new interview; only to be told that it was the same job they had offered me the month before in the shop. This time I accepted out of frustration. I had to do something, so the following Monday I was placed with the company. The first week I spent in a classroom doing maths, stocktaking and learning how to place orders. Then the second week, I started working in a shop. I had only been on the course for twelve days, when my brother Liam offered to take me kitchen fitting. At first I said, "no I can't, I am not even sure how to hold a saw properly". But he insisted that everything would be OK, so I accepted.

I learned that I had a good aptitude for working with wood, even though I was so nervous, that I had many sleepless nights. After a week on the job, I phoned my bank and explained my situation, saying that I would now able to pay off the money I owed them in a few weeks and they were quite happy with the new arrangements.

I then phoned my sister, who told me that I should get in touch with my bank straight away, as they had sent a letter to my mother asking where I was and if I did not start paying off my debt they would be forced to take me to court. So it would seem that my circumstances changed just at the right time.

I would have had all the money paid off quickly, but as the money came in I went out drinking, often very heavily. By Christmas of that year I was working on and off as a carpenter with Liam whenever he thought we could get away with it, but with each new job there were new people and new problems to deal with. I was always afraid that someone would find out that I wasn't a trained carpenter, a 'fake'; especially at the beginning of each new job where I would end up having several sleepless nights.

On a few jobs, I worked with my younger brother Neil, who was also a carpenter. He started to call me a "Paranoid Android" (**Hitch Hikers' Guide to the Galaxy**). I was always wondering if my work was good enough, or if I had been producing enough work. The thing is, none of my bosses ever complained and I was never sacked.

So it seemed that the vivid dream I'd had of my brother Liam dying some six months before had as the book stated 'caused my life to change'.

I was going regularly to Spiritualist Churches and was again invited to join a psychic development circle. In some ways, it helped fill the deep need I had, that there most be more to this life.

Around February 1989, I got my first job working on a cruise liner. It had had a refit several months before, but the company doing it had run out of an edging strip that went around some panels on the staircase, so my job was to remove the panels and put on the new edging and then replace the panels; an easy job.

About a week into the job, I needed some clothes washed, so I went down to the ship's laundry area. As I entered, alarm bells were going off, but everyone was working as normal, so like everyone else I ignored them.

I approached some men and asked loudly,

Why?

"Where can I get my washing done?"
I held up a bag of clothing, the noise from the machines and the alarm bells was so loud that they didn't try to talk, nodding their heads in a negative way, but pointing behind me. I turned around, only to see what looked like a normal metal wall, they must have realised that I had never seen a watertight door before, so one of them went up to a lever, pulled it and a very large metal door started to slowly slide open. When it was open far enough, I stepped through and asked some other crewmembers the same thing.

I got the same response as the others had given, nodding their heads to indicate "No" and pointing back the way I had just come, so I turned around again to find that the watertight door had closed. A quick glance showed that there was another lever on this side of the wall. Stepping forward, I pulled the lever and as the door opened enough I started to step through, not knowing that at the moment I let go of the lever, the door would start to automatically close.

My head and part of my shoulders were through as the door caught me. At first I tried desperately to hold my breath, but the door continued to close. Eventually the pressure violently forced the air out of my lungs. After that, I heard cracking noises as the metal door continued to close. Then everything stopped, I experiencing total peace, there was no up, no down, no light, no dark, no thoughts, no pain, no sense of time or space, just a sense of awareness of 'being'. There was nothing but the peaceful awareness of nothing, of simply being, and it was beautiful.

Another New Beginning

Someone must have pulled the lever to open the door; I staggered through, gasping for breath. My lungs had been constricted and now I could not seem to get any air back into them. I somehow managed to stay on my feet. I staggered further away from the door, eventually bumping into, of all bloody things, a washing machine. By now I was surrounded by people trying to talk to me, but I couldn't hear or understand them, as all my efforts were on trying to breathe. My next memory was of walking with the aid of several people into the ship's medical centre.

  The Doctor kept asking questions as he examined me. I could not answer, as the force of the air leaving my body earlier had hurt my throat so much that I could hardly speak and I was still having problems with my breathing and a bit of shock. The ship's doctor did some x-rays and found that I hadn't even a fractured rib, but he decided that I should go ashore at the next port, which would be Agadir in Morocco, for some more x-rays.

  A few days later we docked at Agadir. The ship arranged transport to a small medical practice, which was run by a happy, heavily accented Portuguese doctor. Unfortunately, he seemed to be the only member of the staff to speak some English, but with some smiling and a lot of exaggerated hand movements, the x-rays were taken.

  Then the usual long wait to see the doctor. Eventually I was ushered into his room by a smiling nurse who good-naturedly pointed to a chair for me to

Why?

sit on. The doctor was several meters away with his back towards me, checking the X-rays.

When he had finished he turned and walked towards me reading a letter the ship's doctor had written. As he got to my side he shot me a quick, surprised look, then straight back to the letter.

He bent slightly, pointing to a sentence he had just read, saying, "The watertight doors can easily cut a man in half".

I shrugged my shoulders.

"Yes."

"Aaah, God, he is a very good friend of yours, no?"

At that we both started to laugh.

The doctor pronounced me fit and healthy with no fractures, only some painful bruising, which ran diagonally from my left shoulder to the bottom of the ribs, with a matching bruise on my back.

Feeling somewhat happier, I returned to the ship and the following day resumed some light work. Several days later, one of the men who had opened the door came up to me in the crew bar wagging his finger and saying with a very strong Oriental accent,

"You velee lucky man. You velee lucky man. You have new rife (life). You live new rife. Velee good man."

He introduced me to a few of the people that were there that day, I thanked them and got them some beer, all of them telling me how lucky I was and how shocked some of them were to have witnessed what had happened.

Another New Beginning

It was an event that I would contemplate on for a long time, it took away my fear of dying, leaving me with the belief that it is for those who are left behind to deal with death and sometimes, the shocking way that death can take a person. If what I experienced was what is called a near-death experience, then it was a very painless and peaceful one, but not for the living that had to witness it.

Several days later when I was feeling better, I went through the watertight door to prove to myself that I was not afraid, although I was a bit apprehensive; but not enough to stop me.

Years later, I found that the cruise company had had an investigation and changed their policy towards contractors. making sure that they were all made aware of the danger of watertight doors.

For much of the past year I had been going regularly to the Spiritualist Church in Southampton, and had also been sitting in a psychic circle (to hopefully develop psychic skills). At first I thought that the mediums were great, but a year on I started to notice the flaws in the messages they gave to people. So often they were so vague that they could fit anyone's life.

I wasn't the only one to notice. After the service, people would stand around chatting and I often heard people saying.

"Well, that message could have been for me."

Which led me to look closer at what was being said and done. There were very few people that I thought were good. Some seemed to be living on what could only be describe as another planet and some were just

Why?

so vague, I wondered if they were in the same room as every one else. Then I noticed that the ones that I considered the best were often simply more confident in their delivery, but they all did one thing in common, they gave comfort and hope and that was why I kept going.

I was starting to form my own beliefs, in part, based on what was happening in the church, also the many books I was reading on the subject of spirituality, but it was never enough to fill the emptiness of my life and as I was earning more money I was binge drinking most weekends. Often I was unable to wake on Monday mornings and no matter how much I tried to put into practice the meditations the books described, I knew that it was not changing me, as I was still very angry inside and no matter how hard I tried, I could not stop drinking or smoking.

Fortunately, I would spend long periods between jobs and during those gaps I would not drink quite so heavily, but I would be just coasting along in life, hopping that fate would take a hand in giving me what I needed. I had always found it very difficult to phone around for work, as just one or two negative responses would be enough to send me into a state of depression. I would only really start to call around when I was almost broke or had already gone overdrawn with the bank. Desperation mixed with depression would become the driving force. It would be then that I got a job, but it would almost always come from a different direction to the one I had been looking, rightly or wrongly reinforcing my belief that fate would give me what I needed. It seemed that the more I trusted that something would happen, the more I got a job just in time to stop me being overdrawn.

My brothers often put pressure on me to take on more work so that I would have less financial problems. They thought that I was lazy. How could I explain to them that I was afraid, when even I did not understand the fear and stresses I was feeling. Although I had tried to change how I behaved, only alcohol seemed to deal with how I felt, allowing me, for a short time, to more easily express myself.

Why?

Chapter five
Am I sane?

By 1989 I had become concerned by what I thought was wrong with the Spiritualist Churches and felt that I had two choices, either to get more involved or to give it up completely. With each passing month, I was becoming more torn. I had seen, both in the army and on construction sites, people getting promotion and they all became part of the system, no matter how idealistic they had been before. I did not want to become part of the problem but I couldn't see a third option. I had too many experiences and too many strange coincidences to dismiss spirituality altogether.

It wasn't hard for me to understand that if I joined the organisation, my ideals would have to change. This, I knew, would be a problem and I already had enough to deal with, but I was also desperate to be a part of something that would help to fill my feeling of loneliness.

I had just got back to Southampton after having another job working away, when I met Charles near to where I was living. He had been going to the same psychic development group as I had. Although we had never spoken, I had witnessed him on several occasions giving other members of the group 'messages', using his psychic abilities, from which I noticed he seemed to get lots of nodding agreement from the recipients. After we had exchanged pleasantries, I asked if he would join me at a nearby cafe for a tea.

After we had been served and I was happy that no one could hear, I asked,

"How is the psychic circle going?"

"Yeah, it's very good. Were you still here when the two women joined the group?"

"Well two new women were there the last night before I went away."

" What did you think about them?"

"Well, they where both quite attractive, but I only saw them once."

He then leaned in and spoke in a whisper,

"We all knew each other in a previous life."

I did not know how to answer that, so there were a few moments of silence.

"We all worked as temple priests, and you were married to one of them."

"Which one?", I asked, buying into his Mills and Boon story.

"I don't know, but the other became so jealous of your relationship that she murdered you, but I don't know which one was which!"

"How do you know this?"

"I saw it."

"Then why don't you know which one is which?"

"I couldn't see them clearly, I just know it was them."

I had been leaning in as well, but now I sat back.

Why?

I felt very uncomfortable with what he had told me and I should have dismissed what he had said, but he had hit on my deepest feeling of loneliness, filling it with an empty hope and I was so desperate for something in my life that went along with his story. Fortunately, work was taking me away from Southampton so regularly that I did not see much of them, but every time I thought of what he had said, or whenever I was around the two women he had spoken about, I was left in a little turmoil. Over the following months, I started to have more contact with Charles. I should have known to back off when he told me that he had been into Voodoo for almost thirty years, but I thought it's the person that makes a thing bad, not the other way around.

After a time, I started to notice some strange things about Charles. As I was not the most talkative person, I would simply listen in on group conversation. Charles had a knack of slipping things into a conversation; it was difficult to describe how he did it, but a small innocent sentence or a single word was enough to leave people feeling confused. He could lift a person up, then knock them down. So I started to avoid him, realising that he had caused the same confusion in me, but I watched from what I thought was a safe distance. One evening he came up to me in the church and said,

"You are attracted to one of the two girls from the psychic group".

I did not answer.

"All you have to do is say so and she can be yours."

In a panic I blurted out

Am I Sane?

"No".

The force of my answer surprised both of us. I did not understand the exact meaning of what he was offering, but a part of me knew that I could never own someone else. "She can be yours" — insinuating that he could somehow manipulate her free will.

Not long after that, my experiences with Charles came to a very dramatic end.

The Spiritualist Church was almost empty and I was sitting near the centre aisle, one row from the back. I was surprised when a man I had known came in looking great and healthy, as only a few weeks before he was in hospital with cancer and supposedly dying.

When the medium part of the service started, the medium went to Charles. He was to my right and in the back corner beside the man with the cancer.

The medium started to say that Charles was a great man and that he possessed great spiritual power. She went on for about five minutes about his wonderful power and his strong healing hands. A man behind me tapped me on the shoulder and as I part turned, he asked in a whisper,

"Is that Spirit talking?"

At that time I believed that spirits were there to help people, but not to boost their ego, I said with a frown,

"No, it can't be".

As I went to turn back I looked over at Charles and the man with the cancer, they were both looking directly at me, insanely smiling and nodding their heads more like rabid dogs than men. Frightened by what I had just

Why?

seen I turned away to my left. There was a picture on the wall of Jesus kneeling and praying. I started praying to it, as now I could feel an energy around me, I felt as if something was trying to break me.

As I looked at the picture of Jesus, the only thing I could think was,

"Please, I don't know how to love, you must send them love. Don't send them back the pain they wish on me, please just send them love".

I am not sure how long it went on for, but the whole thing was broken when a lady in the front row stood up. She was looking at the same picture of Jesus. "Look at that. It's so beautiful!", she said

No one seemed to notice what she had said, but at that moment the intense feeling that was around me stopped and so did the medium/physic part of the service.

I then had to stand, as a hymn had started. I was trembling so much that I had to lean on the chair in front of me. Although I was shaken, I decided that I would not rush away and hide from what I had just experienced; there was always, some tea after the service. Fortunately, the shaking had stopped by the time I picked up the cup of tea, so I downed it quickly and left without speaking to anyone. By the time I got home I felt exhausted and fell into bed.

When I woke the next morning I felt cleaner than I ever had, even the air somehow seemed fresher. Everything seemed different and clean.

The following week I returned to the church, even that seemed to have changed. Charles and the man with cancer were gone and everything seemed so normal that I seriously started to doubt my own sanity. Had I lost the plot, had I just imagined everything that had happened with Charles over the past several months?

For a while, I seriously doubted my own sanity, although at the same time, I felt as if a heaviness had been lifted from my mind.

I have never met Charles again. I was told some months later that he had left the city and the man with cancer had died shortly afterwards.

Four years later, I was able to speak to the woman who had stood up. At first she was very reluctant to tell me what had happened. I told her that I also was having an inner experience when she stood up.

Eventually she told me that as she looked at the picture of Jesus,

"He was standing with his arms by his side, palms outwards and that it was just beautiful".

The actual picture we where both looking at that night is of Jesus side on, kneeling and praying, not standing.

During the time with Charles, I had also been going to a healing group, which was just along the same road from the Spiritualist Church. I had heard about it more than a year before, but I had been told that it was by invite only. The group was run by a Mrs. Murdock, who was well into her seventies. She was well known and highly regarded within the spiritual circles as a healer, having been doing it for almost fifty years. Her living room and dining room were used for the healing and about twenty people turned up each week, some to be

Why?

healers and others to be healed. At first, everything seemed to be what I expected, which was that I could not tell if anything was actually happening. At one point I was asked if I would like to help one of the healers channel some energy for a "lady patient". There were four chairs in a row, each with a patient; a healer at the front and another behind. Not knowing what to do, I just stood behind the lady and put my hands on her shoulders and to my surprise and bewilderment they became unnaturally hot. The healer stood in front of her patient and moved her hands over her as if wiping something away. This went on for about ten or fifteen minutes, then the healer said gently to her with a smile,

"We're finished now".

The patient then turned to me and said,

"Thank you, that was very pleasant".

A little confused I replied,

"Ah yeah!"

I really wasn't sure if anything had happened.

An hour and a half later, all except one person had had healing. I was sitting on the couch in the living room area watching what had or had not been going on, the person sitting beside me leaned in saying in a whisper,

"Mrs. Murdock is going to do her trance healing now".

She came into the living room and pointed to a lady that had been doing healing earlier.

"Will you come and help?"

Without answering, she was on her feet and heading towards her.

Am I Sane?

As if the night had not been strange enough, what then transpired was even stranger. Mrs. Murdoch began by standing in front of her patient, closing her eyes and taking a deep breath. She started making strange, low sounds that kind of sounded Oriental, she then started moving her hands over her patient as she continued to make the Oriental sounds. This went on for about ten minutes. I was both intrigued and disturbed, wanting to understand what was going on, but at the same time, feeling that it was just one hell of a show she had just put on. Then the whole thing was finished off with a cup of tea and biscuits, there's nothing quite like a bit of civilisation mixed in with insanity.

By now, all the things to do with channeling, healing and Tarot cards had disillusioned me. People who claim to do trance mediumship, I had come to believe, were in some way controlled schizophrenics. I had come across and known several of them over the past few years and had come to believe that they had split their own personalities, creating an alter ego that would be able to say many of the things they would normally be too afraid of saying. In all the time that I had spent in spiritual churches, I found only two mediums that I respected (and both of them are no longer involved with the churches) and only one good Tarot card reader. I still felt there was something there, so I held on to the hope that there was something more that could help others without me even thinking, I did that, or Spirit channeled that *through me*.

The one exceptional Tarot reader was a woman named Margaret; she did it to help people, as she was

Why?

fortunate not to need to do it for money. She helped more on a psychological level and made several predictions about my future, all of which happened – that I was about to get into a relationship, the girl's birth sign, that I would be going away soon and I would earn a lot of money.

She also insisted that I should practice smiling, something that I was not good at (being happy). A blank expression was about all I could usually muster. This was probably the best piece of advice anyone had ever given me. I had walked around with a blank look on my face for such a long time.

Margaret told me I should at least experiment, to go to a place I had not been to and try smiling. What did I have to lose? So I went to a pub, and tried to genuinely smile and feel it inside.

To my surprise, I found that the barmaid stopped to talk, then a couple on the bar stools next to me started chatting. This actually seemed to work, so I decided to practice smiling. I found it hard at first, as it was so easy to have no expression. I would simply walk down the high street with a small smile and whenever I saw someone frowning, it reminded me to smile and I would mentally thank them for the reminder. It took a long time, but did become easier and easier, as smiling became a part of me.

Some two months later I met Elaine, a girl who just happened to have the birth sign that the Tarot reader had predicted and I seemed to be going on the job she had predicted as well. Unfortunately the latter was in Germany. But my brothers, Neil and Liam, and my Uncle Joe were also all on this job. It was originally only meant to be for three weeks, but it ended up lasting for three months, with only a short break for Christmas and New Year.

During the first few weeks in Germany I phoned my new girlfriend often, not always getting an answer. Elaine said that her young daughter had been pulling the plug on her phone, which seemed like a reasonable explanation.

Germany is a wonderful place to be if you like to have drink. It doesn't matter what time of the day or night it was, there's always somewhere open; a far cry from the restrictions in the UK at the time. I didn't think that I was drinking heavily, but my brother Liam did. When we returned to the hotel early one morning he turned to me as he was about to enter his room and said,

"Why are you trying to drink yourself into oblivion?"

Surprised, I didn't answer; I just stood there looking at him, waiting for him to give an explanation. Fortunately, he turned and entered his room, leaving me standing on my own in the hotel corridor. I looked at his closed door, not thinking, but trying to feel what was inside of me, all that was there was a cold dark empty determination. When I was drinking, it was easy to forget to smile.

I turned and walked to my room, focusing on that emptiness, finding a strength in it. That night I had been drinking far more than Liam – two, sometimes three to his one; it had become so normal for me. I knew

Why?

that there was truth in what he had said but there was nothing I could do about it and no matter how I tried to stop, I found it impossible.

We all went home for Christmas. The day I got home I went down with flu until the day I went back to Germany, so I did not see much of my girlfriend.

I spent another two months in Germany earning lots of money, but it became too much with my girlfriend. The phone would be engaged too many times and I hated the feelings that it brought up in me; confusion, uncertainty and then jealousy. Then I started to think that I was just like the people from my past. That became the most difficult part, as the more there was no answer from my phone calls, the more I began to hate myself for what I was thinking and feeling. I could not face the thought that I might be like Benny or my father. Fortunately, drinking heavily was a good way to offset the feeling. When the job ended and I returned to the UK I saw her once and knew that I could not face the feelings that being with her caused, it was better to run away than face the idea that I might become what I hated.

With the money I earned, I got a little car and spent two months off work. The mornings were spent in walking several miles just for something to do, then in the afternoon I spent one hour trying to meditate. Doing this, even though I wasn't very successful, did seem to help me to relax and not spend as much time in the pub. Most Thursdays and Sundays I went to the Spiritualist Church, but only got an increasing feeling that there was little spirituality there. I went to Mrs. Murdock's healing centre on two more occasions. At the end of the second night, she came into the living room and pointed at me.

"Will you please come and do the healing with me tonight?"

As I stood up, my left shoulder felt as if it had a sudden jerk and seemed to become dislocated, the whole arm dropping several inches. I reached over with my right hand as I thought,

"I am not the doer ".

As I lifted and pulled the arm, it slipped painlessly back into position. I took my place behind the patient and put my hands on her shoulders, allowing my mind to go blank, again my hands became unnaturally hot. Mrs. Murdock started by closing her eyes and taking a deep breath. When she opened them again, she started to seemingly speak in an oriental language. I stood impassively watching the bizarre show in front of me as she started waving her hands in front of her patient. She brushed the ends of my fingers on my left hand, then she pulled away very sharply, as if she had been burnt. Drawing her breath in fast and loudly, the end of my fingers, where she had touched me, had become icy cold, although the rest of the fingers stayed very hot, as if a line had been drawn across them. I did not react, my mind stayed in the peaceful place it had been in until Mrs. Murdock had finished. I left the room heading for the kitchen and sat down straight away. This I needed to think about, but Mrs. Murdock followed me in.

"You should come to the healing more often"

Why?

At this point I went into a whole new level of madness, because I could hear another voice as clear as day in my ear, but this one had no body.

"How would she know?"

"Their have been many occasions in the past where people have been cured of serious diseases", said Mrs. Murdock.

"Go on then, ask her what it tastes like."

"I have performed surgery on patients to remove cancer."

"Well ask her."

"Tumors."

"Ask her, did it taste nice?"

As the list of what she had done got longer, the disembodied voice persisted in telling me to ask how it tasted. I sat there in a numb silence, there was no way I was going to answer either of them. When Mrs. Murdock had finished talking, the voice did the same, which was fortunate, as I had been seriously doubting my own sanity since my experience with Charles and this was not helping.

I left after a cup of tea, deciding to never go back. I never saw Mrs. Murdock again and fortunately, I never heard from the disembodied voice either.

I was beginning to notice that my love affair with alcohol had a rhythm, the more I worked, the more I drank and there were two types of evenings. One was sitting alone just watching the clock behind the bar, timing myself a rum and coke, roughly every 10-15 minutes. The other evenings, I would go on a pub-crawl,

Am I Sane?

always aware that for some reason, I was looking for something, but not knowing what it was. I found myself rushing from one pub to another. I would order one drink, look around and before it was served, I knew that whatever it was that I wanted wasn't here, so I would quickly finish the drink and walk or, if it was getting late, run to the next pub. That's how I spent most Fridays and Saturdays, or more if I could afford it.

It was now the beginning of May and an itch to get a job was becoming too much. My brothers were becoming relentless in their nagging (concern) that I get a job. So reluctantly, I made a few calls and was surprised to get a call offering me a job that was due to start in two weeks, fitting out a hotel in Ghana, Africa. The strange thing was, that I had never worked for the agency before and my two brothers had never heard of them either. All I would have to do was send them my passport and they would arrange the visa and flights. Then I just had to wait for the company to call with the flight details, but the following Monday, the call I got was bad news; the contract had been cancelled and the whole thing was off. My hopes had been so high, as the whole situation fitted in so nicely with what I was trying to believe, so now I really needed some direction.

I had heard of a medium by the name of Chris Harris, his name always seemed to come up when people talked about good mediums and it just so happened that he would be at the local Spiritualist Church on Thursday night, so I went along.

During the mediumistic part of the service he turned and pointed to me,

Why?

"Don't worry. That job you want is yours and you'll be OK with money".

That was all he said before turning to someone else.

I left thinking, "What does he know?"

At that time, there was only that one job and that was off, but to my surprise and joy the following Monday morning, the company phoned and asked if I was still interested in going to Africa; of course I said yes.

When the day I arrived, I had with me the last of my money, twenty pounds; or should I say the last of my overdraft. But I was soon financially sound again, and, I had a great time there. The Ghanaians are a happy bunch of people, who like a good laugh, but who always seemed to want me to meet their sisters, as they thought that I should be married. In their culture, to still be single at my age, 26, is considered very, very bad.

So at one point, for a laugh I said, look,

"I am going to wait till I am around 70-80 years old, then marry an 18-year-old and die happy".

I was very surprised that they actually believed me, saying,

"No, no Mr. Joe that is very bad. You will be dirty old man, very bad, don't do it".

I was a bit surprised that they believed me so I thought I would play it up. For several days, strangers kept coming up to me on the job saying,

"Mr. Joe, you can't do it, you'll be dirty old man. It's very bad, don't do it! I have a nice sister, come and meet her!"

The first time it happened, I had no idea what they were talking about. I just stared before comprehension

Am I Sane?

finally dawned on me. It had been such a long time since I had laughed so much. After that, I would just smile and walk off, leaving them to think what they wanted.

I did become very sick there on several occasions. Twice with diarrhea and on one occasion the flu, at least the doctor said it was, as it was by far the worst flu I had ever had and the diarrhea, if it wasn't so bad it would have been almost comical, but I won't go into that.

By the time I returned to the UK it was late August 1990, a week before I was due to arrive back in Southampton, and found I had nowhere to live.

My brothers Liam and Neil had decided they could no longer afford to pay the mortgage on the house, so decided to rent it out. Unfortunately they were unable to contact me in Africa. Luckily my other brother, Mick, said that I could stay in his flat with his family for a few days until I found somewhere new to live.

I had arrived back in Southampton on a Saturday, so started looking for accommodation, but by Thursday I took to bed feeling ill. By Saturday I had a severe fever, and by Sunday morning I was virtually lying in a pool of my own sweat.

I was admitted to Southampton General Hospital's Contagious Diseases Department. By now I had a temperature of 104. I was going from bouts of extreme sweating to shivering and felt as though someone was hitting me in the head with a hammer, strangling me, sitting on my chest, punching me in the stomach and kicking me between the legs. Blood tests had been taken the moment I arrived, but proved to be inconclusive. My

Why?

brother later told me that the doctors believed that I had Malaria, although no parasite had been found in my blood. However, they suspected that I may have another disease as well, because my symptoms were so severe. So they would not be treating me until more conclusive blood tests could be done. Sure enough, a malaria parasite was found, but nothing else and I was finally given quinine to kill it off. The quinine worked extremely fast and I was released on Friday morning with another week's supply.

It also happened that the week I came home from Africa, my mother had travelled down from Scotland for a holiday, so she spent most of her holiday visiting me in hospital. A day after I was released from hospital, she travelled back home.

I moved back into my brother Mick's flat, but it was obvious that his wife was very uncomfortable with me being there. She was obviously afraid that I might pass on some "African disease" to her two young children. So I felt I should move out as soon as possible.

A year earlier I had been working in Cornwall in the South of England and had gone to a Spiritualist Church. The medium that night was Ashley, a very flamboyant character, dressed almost all in white, something that would normally have put me off straight away, but what he said to people was very direct. In all the church services I had been to so far, there had been no mediums that evoked such a positive response from the people to whom they were giving a psychic message too.

I did not manage to speak to him that night but I returned to Cornwall several months later just to have a talk with him. Our conversation was very brief, although he gave me his phone number and said,

"If ever you need help or someone to talk to, just call".

So now I called him. He asked how I was doing and I explained about the Malaria. He immediately invited me down. He had just opened a restaurant with his friend Chris. At first I said,

"No, thank you," because I had realised on my last visit that he was gay and sharing a house did not seem like a good idea to me. But that afternoon, I found my bag sitting beside the front door. It may have been nothing, but I felt uncomfortable, however, the following morning I called Ashley again and accepted his offer and drove down that morning to Cornwall.

Ashley and Chris fed me from their restaurant and I would take long walks, sometimes with Ashley. We would talk of God, spirit, energy, just about everything.

I was surprised that after the first day, Ashley told me that he and Chris were partners. To me that had been very obvious when we met at his house earlier in the year. By mid-week, Ashley almost scared me off by telling me that he loved me. I explained that although I thought he was a great guy, I was not that way inclined. Fortunately he did not go on about it. I now think he was just trying to see my reaction by throwing something unexpected into the conversation

The following morning, Chris and Ashley went for provisions for the restaurant. I thought very hard about what Ashley had said the night before, often thinking that I should just leave, but I decided to put

Why?

aside my own fear and insecurities and stay, because I had a very deep feeling that there was something that I needed to learn from them.

When they returned, they were surprised to see me. Ashley had told Chris what had happened and said that he would not be too surprised if I was gone.

It was that night that the conversation took a fateful turn. Chris asked me,

"Have you ever heard of a holy man called Sai Baba?"

"I have heard of some so called Indian holy men, but from what I have seen so far I'm not in the slightest bit impressed by any of them."

He then went on to tell me of his experiences with Sai Baba, in that they had been living in a cottage on a farm when Sai Baba appeared to Chris one night in his bedroom and said,

"What do you want for you to believe in me?"

"Make it snow", replied Chris.

He then fell back to sleep, only to be woken the next morning hearing Ashley screaming in the kitchen, so he rushed down to find that in his garden — and only there — was a covering of snow, in the middle of summer.

He told me the story in such a casual way that by the time he had finished, my head was tilting to one side and my mouth was open.

I had believed some stupid things over the years and it looked like I was about to add another one to the list, because the way he told this story seemed to have a truth about it. I also hoped that to some extent I could now tell the difference between the truth and a lie, this

Am I Sane?

man totally believed what he was saying and he still managed to look and sound sane. This was a bit far-fetched even for me, although the way he told his story stopped me dismissing it as nonsense. They then showed me a video of this Sai Baba. He was quite short and his hair was more life an African's than an Indian's. He was wearing a long sleeved, one piece orange robe as he walked around a large group of people that were sitting cross-legged on the ground. Twice he stopped and started to wave his hand in a circular motion, then he seemed to give something to a person in the crowd.

I asked, Chris,

"What's he doing?"

"He's producing an ash called Vibhuti; it's the Hindu equivalent of holy water."

"Producing?" I said.

"Yes, it just appears from the palm of his hand."

Ha! I thought, now is a good time to be quiet.

This looked too much like sleight of hand, but out of politeness I did not mention my skepticism about this small strange man in an orange robe.

When the video finished we sat in the living room and they talked about Sai Baba and the people that they know who had gone to India to see him, but there was only one thing that Chris said of him that would stay with me.

"Of all the people we have known who have been to see him, all have changed in one way or another."

Of all the things they could have said this one remark stuck in my mind. It was the one thing I needed to hear more than anything else — he changed people. As

Why?

long as I could remember, I had desperately wanted to change and had been unable too.

After that night, I put all thought of this Sai Baba aside; I had more pressing problems that I was trying to avoid. And there was no way I was ever going to India.

I had spent just over a week with Chris and Ashley; I felt that I was getting stronger by the day. By the end of my time with them, I found that a friend in Southampton would put me up in her spare room. So I had somewhere to live, but again I did not phone for work, hoping that something would come to me.

When I returned to Southampton, I spent the next month and a half recovering. Each day I would do a short meditation and each night have a few drinks, but not binge drinking, just enough to get to sleep.

During that time, I joined yet another psychic development group. The woman who ran it, finding out I worked as a carpenter, asked me to make a massage bed. I wasn't keen on the idea, but she gave me a Tarot reading, insisting that I was to start my own business making and selling them and I could make the first one for her.

Unfortunately it backfired on her, as the first one I made wasn't really that good; it was not until I made the second one that I found out what a proper portable massage bed should look like. But time and money were not on my side. I eventually sold the second and third one about six months later. You just can't trust a good Tarot reader can you!

As I was running out of money, I asked my brother Mick for a loan, but he was not in a state to help,

Am I Sane?

so I got down to 50 pounds in the bank. No job and no money coming in. When the same brother came to my place asking if I still needed some money, of course I said, "Yes". He then gave me a cheque for nearly £200. When I looked closer at it, it had been written by the last company that I worked for and it was my first pay cheque that they had sent six months before. My sister-in-law had misplaced it; I immediately put it in the bank. It cleared by Friday and I was very careful not to spend anything unwisely.

Then Monday morning, my brother Mick turned up at my door and asked me if I was interested in starting a job with him. I was more than just interested, especially now as it was November, traditionally the worst time of the year for the building industry, and I hadn't worked for almost three months. Things had been getting worse, even for my brothers, because the UK was in yet another recession. So I said,

"Yes, when do we start?"

He smiled and said,

"Well, there is one small catch; we have to leave at 6 o'clock tonight for Euro Disney in France".

Now there was a mad rush on, fortunately the money I now had in the bank was just enough to buy new working boots and some winter working clothes. November in Paris was very cold and we would be working very long hours.

We thought we would be working ten-hour days, but most days we would work twelve. As we got closer to Christmas, we occasionally worked 14 hours a day in sub-zero temperatures, so not much time for anything

Why?

other than a meal, a shower then back to bed. Sundays we had off, so I would get seriously drunk Saturday night and Sunday, which meant that I would have some Mondays off, as I was incapable of getting out of bed.

The job closed down over Christmas, but no one had been informed if there would be any work in the New Year. By then, I had saved £1,400, but the next two weeks I spent almost all of my time in bars, and the rest I guess I spent irresponsibly. During the Christmas and New Year period I drank much more than normal, paying little attention to how much I was spending. It was after all the festive season and I was trying to drink myself into happiness, having given up on Spiritual Churches and all that they entailed. I felt more lost than usual and in the back of my mind I knew that I would continue to be unemployed going into the new year, as the building industry seemed to be virtually dead. So, I guess I was drinking to ignore the reality of my life, searching for happiness in bars and nightclubs.

As I was recovering from the New Year hangover, the company I had been working for phoned Mick, offering us seven days' work back at Euro Disney. I was nearly broke and there was no other work around, so I gladly accepted.

The first week into the job, Mick managed to dislocate his shoulder by falling over and was sent home. I, on the other hand ended up working longer hours, often from seven thirty in the morning till nine at night. The company's attitude was, well if you don't like the hours you can leave! We were issued with high-vis vests with numbers on the back. After a few days, it became apparent why, when several people where sacked. The management were using the numbers on our backs as an easy way of recognising individuals they saw not working from a distance, then they would send out the foremen to dismiss then, knowing that there was little chance of work back home.

I ended up fitting the decorative moldings on the roofs. It was quite cold, but fortunately by midday, if I was lucky, it would get a little warmer than for those who had to work inside the building. On a good day, the temperature would rise as high as minus four or even three degrees.

Near the end of the first week, the main contractor called all the carpenters together and informed us that we would be needed for another seven days — which was great, financially. As I was walking away I turned to one of the other carpenters saying,

"If I get £2000 in the bank, I'm going to India".

But there was a bit I was thinking that I did not say as I finished the sentence,

"To see this Sai Baba".

Almost as soon as I said it I dismissed the thought — a good idea but unrealistic.

At the end of each week, all the workers were gathered together to be told if we would be working the following week and each time we were informed that there would be one more week. The longer the job went on, the more I told the other workers that I would go to India if I managed to save £2000, although I never really believed it myself. I knew I was never going to get £2000.

Why?

I was still buying a bottle of vodka or rum to drink at the weekends, sitting on my own on an evening. Unfortunately, it meant that I only managed to work four or five (mostly five) days, rather than the six days a week I was supposed to be doing.

Some of the lads would tell me that they had tried to wake me, but I was dead to the world. I would eventually come round at about ten or twelve o'clock, but even then I was still not capable of doing much.

The first of March was a Monday and the seven-day job had gone on now for over two months, but this morning would be my last. I woke up around 10 o'clock suffering from yet another hangover, but this time it was different. I was so ashamed of having yet another day off through alcohol abuse, that the moment I woke up and realised what I had done, I decided to go to India. It was the only reasonable excuse that I had to get away from the embarrassment of having yet another day off through alcohol. I couldn't face the looks that I knew people would give me at work.

Anyway, I had told enough people that if I got £2000 I would be going, so now I had the money and was embarrassed enough that I was prepared to go all the way to India, just to hide the fact that I had a drink problem.

First I had to go to work and inform my employers. As I walked down Disney Main Street, several people called out,

"Hey Joe, were you drunk again this morning?"

I put on the best smile I could, "No I've got the money, so I've decided this morning to go to India", trying my best not to show how hung over I was.

Am I Sane?

I left France that afternoon for Southampton and by Wednesday morning I was trying to find out about flights and visas. Although I still did not know the whereabouts in India of Sai Baba, as I had misplaced Ashley's phone number, I was looking at prices for Calcutta or New Delhi – after all I thought, "How difficult could it be to find one holy man in India?"

Fortunately, on Wednesday afternoon, I went into town and met Steve Smith, whom I had known from a Spiritualist Church. We hadn't seen each other for about two years. We exchanged pleasantries and asked each other what we had been doing. I tried a bit of spiritual one-upmanship by telling him,

"I am going to India to see a holy man called Sai Baba".

But to my surprise he said very casually,

"Oh I was there last year, and had a great time".

"Please can I get you a tea and you can at tell me were he lives!"

Steve told me that Baba lived in an ashram called Prasanthi Nilayam, which was in a small town called Puttaparthi, about a four-hour taxi drive from Bangalore City.

I felt very fortunate that I happened to bump into him just before I was about to book my flights. It seemed like a good omen for what was to come. By Friday night, I had a visa and a flight to New Delhi, I would be buying an internal flight from Delhi to Bangalore, so I would be leaving the UK on the tenth of March, not bad considering I had only left France ten days before.

Why?

Chapter Four

Sai Baba

The sun had just risen when the plain landed in New Delhi and as soon as the exit door was opened, the dry heat quickly started to warm the cabin. With a stopover in Dubai, the journey so far had taken over seventeen hours. I hadn't slept for close to a day and a half, so I was feeling a bit rough. I shuffled forward with the other passengers down the narrow isle towards the exit, bright sunshine streamed through the door and the closer I got, the warmer it felt. On exiting, I had to momentarily squint, as my eyes adjusted to the intense sunshine. The heat felt good, but after only a few moments I was already looking forward to getting into the shade of the terminal. I expected the building to be cooler, but it was stiflingly hot; the air seemed to be stale. I followed the signs for arrivals, clearing customs quickly, then headed for the baggage collection area. Changing some money, I asked about domestic flights and was told I could get a bus to the domestic airport. On exiting the arrivals area, I was approached by a well-dressed Indian man.

"Can I help you sir?"

"No thanks", I replied without really looking at him, as I looked around trying to see signs for a bus service to the domestic airport.

"Where are you going to sir?"

"Bangalore", hoping that would put him off.

"I can help you with that."

I stopped, as I seemed to be getting nowhere looking for a bus.

"Ok, where do I get the bus?"

"This way sir."

I let him lead me to a counter, where he had a conversation with another man in his own language.

"When did you want to go sir?"

"Today", I replied.

Some more conversation entailed and a few moments on a computer.

"I am sorry sir, there is no flight today to Bangalore. There is one tomorrow morning and if you will allow me, I can arrange the flight, a good hotel and a taxi to get you back to the airport in time for your flight in the morning."

"How much?"

A short time later I had a flight ticket and was on my way to a small hotel, which was an hour's drive in the opposite direction, away from the city.

So after a night in a hotel, I resumed my trip to Bangalore, arriving at midday on the 12th. Steve had advised me that I should order a pre-

Why?

paid taxi from within the airport. I did as my friend had said and got the taxi, just saying,

"Take me to Sai Baba's ashram".

Just over thirty minutes later, the taxi stopped outside two very large metal gates, which were attached to similarly large walls. To one side of the gates was a sign.

'BRINDAVAN'.

Whitefield.

The driver got out and started to remove my bags.

"HEY, what are you doing?"

With a frown, he pointed to the gates,

"Sai Baba's ashram".

"No, no, this can't be Sai Baba's ashram."

"Yes, yes, Sai Baba."

"Noo, Sai Baba's ashram is FOUR HOURS away."

"Yes, Sai Baba", he said, as he pointed towards the gates.

"This can't be it, Sai Baba lives in a place called Puttaparthi", I said with more force.

"No, no, Sai Baba Ashram; you only pay for here."

By now I was outside the taxi with my rucksack. The driver kept repeating the same thing, with an ever-increasing frown.

"Sai Baba ashram."

Then it dawned on me

"Ooo s—-, maybe there's more than one person called Sai Baba."

And maybe I had just paid a taxi to take me to the wrong one. This place did not in any way fit Steve's description or the video I had seen, and it had only taken me thirty minutes to get here; not four hours.

A little bewildered, I walked into what seemed to be an empty ashram.

I hadn't gone more than 20 paces, when I stopped to look around. The road went straight for another 100 metres, then took a sharp right and carried on for about another 250 metres, before it stopped at another set of gates. On the left side of the road were several three-story buildings that followed the road, to the right an oblong area covered in sand with one large tree and a line of coconut trees running along the external wall.

It was now about two in the afternoon and the temperature was in the mid thirties. The place was deserted; the intense midday sun seemed to make everything sharper; more defined. There was something about it that left me with a deep feeling, that after all the experiences I had in my life, they were nothing compared to this place. Even though there was a strong possibility that I was in the "wrong place".

I had been standing there alone for a few minutes feeling slightly insignificant, when I

Why?

heard footsteps behind me, turning towards them I was surprised to see a young clean shaven European man, dressed all in white.

"Hi, do you need help?", he asked.

I tried to hide my surprise at the white shirt and trousers he was wearing. His accent put him as southern European.

" Is this Sai Baba's ashram?"

"Yes, it is", he replied.

I was still not fully convinced that we were talking about the same Sai Baba, and didn't really want to say to him, "short guy, orange robe, with curly afro hair".

"Well, do you know where I can get some accommodation?"

"The accommodation office is just over there."

He pointed to one of the buildings further up the road on the left. He turned and seemed about to take me there, but I felt a little uncomfortable, I was just not used to anyone being so nice or helpful, especially someone dressed all in white.

"No, it's ok", I said quickly.

"Just point me in the general direction."

On entering the accommodation office a few minutes later, I relaxed, as there were several pictures of Sai Baba on the walls.

"Passport", said the elderly man in the office.

"Swami will not be out to give Darshan for some hours yet", he said, as he took my passport and started filling in some forms.

I nodded, assuming he meant Sai Baba would have a walk around later. So I had some time to settle in.

The room in the ashram cost 10 rupees per night, very good considering I got 48 rupees to the pound, so I could get five nights for just one pound.

The room was basic, with four small cabinets set into the walls, a concrete floor and two mattresses, which were covered by mosquito nets. Compared to some of the places that I had slept in when in the army, it was still luxurious. One of the beds still had a body on it; he introduced himself as Jeff from New Zealand. He told me that I would be able to buy a mosquito net and a mattress outside the ashram after Darshan, when the shops would reopen. The other person in the room would only appear just before lights out, then disappear first thing in the morning.

Jeff explained that Sai Baba had three ashrams; one at Brindavan, near Bangalore, the largest one was in Puttaparthi, Andhra Pradesh and a third small one at a hill station called Kodaikanal.

About 30 to 40 minutes before Sai Baba came out, the ashram started to fill. It seemed that at least a quarter of the people there, were non-Indians from around the world and almost all of

Why?

them were wearing white clothing. Everyone sat in ordered straight lines on the sand near a tree at the front of the ashram. Jeff told me that the people sitting at the front of each line would pick a token from a bag; the token number would determine when their line entered the area where Sai Baba would walk.

Just before five o'clock, Sai Baba came out of his residence. By now there were around 300 people sitting around the tree. Emerging from the tree's lower trunk was a corrugated roof, which went around in the shape of a hexagon, giving some protection from the intense late afternoon sun.

The area around the tree was divided into five sections, two of them for men and the other three for women Each section was separated by a walkway leading to the tree, which was perhaps 150 meters from the entrance of Sai Baba's house.

My first sight of Sai Baba was as he walked around the tree. He had already been walking around for at least five minutes, but I could not see him, because the tree itself blocked my view as he emerged from the compound.

When he did enter my line of sight, I had to stretch to be able to see over the heads of those in front of me. I watched him impassively; the whole thing was rather strange.

Some people were handing him letters and others seemed to be offering him trays of sweets, from which he would grab large handfuls and throw them into the crowd. Adults and children alike grabbed at the sweets enthusiastically. Some seemed a little bit too aggressive for just a sweet.

A few sweets landed around me and one managed to get under my right leg. I lifted my knee and an adult beside me quickly snatched it up, I looked at him in surprise, but his attention was already back to Baba.

Sai Baba quickly disappeared around the other side of the tree, then about ten minutes later, as if on some cue that I was not aware of, everyone stood up. Sai Baba had returned to his compound. The Darshan was over.

I left feeling a bit confused as to what had happened, and a little unimpressed by this rather strange Indian holy man who threw sweets at people; something that I decided then and there, that I wouldn't, in any way, be getting involved with.

I was still prepared to stay and see what would happen. After all I had nowhere else to go!

It seemed that everyone around the ashram was wearing white clothes, which were lightweight, a lot more comfortable than the jeans and t-shirts that I had brought with me, so I conformed and got some white clothes - the only time in my life that I wore something that looked like pyjamas during the day.

Why?

The following morning after breakfast, Swami would have a walk around again. This time I had a plan, I had had a good look at the area that he would be walking around the night before and knew which areas would give the best view, and hopefully I would get closer to one of the walkways. Sai Baba came out of the compound at about 8.30; and I had a much better view as he crossed the sand to get to the tree.

Again he took letters and started to throw sweets into the crowd, again some fell around my legs, but I ignored them and within a few seconds he had passed by me.

When he had gone about another 30 feet, I felt something on my left arm. On looking down, there were two sweets; one oblong, about an inch long and the other thin and square, rolling end over end from the top of my forearm, down into the palm of my hand.

As I watched, I knew that nothing could roll like that naturally. When they eventually stopped in the palm of my hand, my mind had gone numb. I just stared uncomprehendingly at them.

When I looked up, Sai Baba was still at the same place, but he was looking straight at me. Their seemed to be no expression on his face; he was just looking at me. After a few moments, I looked back down at the sweets, my mind still blank, unable to comprehend the strangeness of what had just happened. When I looked up again, Sai Baba had already moved to the other side of the tree and a few minutes later, everyone stood up and started to leave. Baba had left the ashram by way of a car that had been waiting on the other side of the tree. I followed the crowd out of the ashram, with the sweets still in my left hand, part of me wanted to throw them away. My thoughts kept revolving around the look on Baba's face. Usually when I've looked at someone's face, there's always been something that I can understand from his or her facial expressions.

But the look he gave me was not like that. It touched something deep inside, leaving me with a confusing feeling; that I had never been anywhere, never done anything, and had never experienced anything. He touched something deep within me and I just knew that there was something about this man that was different. A part of me just believed in him, but at the same time, I could not help but feel confused. And that frightened part of me was saying,

"What the hell am I doing here?"

The first week I was there, I managed several times to sit near the front. Often Baba would stop in front of me and take letters from people. A Hindu custom I had noticed was people scrambling to touch his feet. This was another strange Indian thing that I was definitely not going to get into, so I would just sit there looking at him not knowing what to do or expect. Then without even looking at me, he would walk off.

Why?

When I was outside, I often asked questions about him and heard amazing stories, but I was confused as to why I was here. What could he do for me? I thought of myself as not a particularly very nice person, so what right did I have to be around him if he was a real Holy Man?

When I got into conversation with the people around the ashram, they would ask me what I wanted from life, so I started to look at what I felt about my past, what I had done, what in my life had given me happiness.

Looking back at my past I observed that so far, nothing had given me happiness. In everything I had done, there was an emptiness, a lack of feeling; it didn't matter what I had become good at or had accomplishedtat the moment of accomplishment I had always felt empty, something was definitely missing. I could not remember being happy, nothing had lasted; it all seemed to be without love. So I decided that what I wanted from life was to "be happy, to love', nothing else really matters.

At the end of the first week I was sitting in the front row, again Baba came and stood in front of me, taking letters from the people behind me.

He was leaning over me so much that I had to lean back so I looked up at him, which started to hurt, so rather than hurt myself I looked down, my eyes stopping on his feet.

I took a gentle breath in through my mouth. I was overcome with awe; everything about his feet seemed to be perfect; beautiful. The experience seemed to permeate my mind, filling the whole body. I marveled at the beauty I was seeing and experiencing. The same word kept repeating softy in my mind,

"Beautiful, beautiful, beautiful".

I have no idea how long he was there, but he must have taken all the letters and started to walk away, which broke the experience. I frowned, my mind momentarily blank, and then it lurched into the most ridiculous explanation.

"Oh my God, I have a foot fetish and never knew itte

Then my mind went back to being numb.

Later I considered more deeply what had happened. It was some sort of inner experience I had been through. I could have been looking at anything and still I would have seen it as perfect and beautiful, as the experience seemed to come from within. Somehow, this Sai Baba had triggered it, but this was too strange for me to talk about and a part of me did not really want to accept what I had experienced.

I was urged by some of the people who had been around the ashram for a while to write a letter to Baba, so I started to think, what is it I want to know?

I had an experience during a meditation the year before that was strange. I had asked myself.

"Who am I?"

"The body!"

Why?

"No, that will die, so I cannot be that."

"My name?"

"That was given to me at birth, so it can't be that."

"The voice in my head that I think things through with?"

"No, it has no substance, no form of its own."

Then, for a moment I had an experience of nothing, emptiness, a void. If it had not been for the fact that I was sitting, I would have fallen over, as my mind tried to lurch away from being enveloped in the emptiness. It was so similar to the experience I had had years before when I was being crushed by the ship's watertight doors; nothingness without the sense of peace.

After the initial shock I thought,

"Surely I am more than nothing, a void?"

But I could feel that I lacked a real sense of me. So here I was a year later in the presence of someone that could possibly explain it to me.

So I started the letter.

"Dear Baba,

Who am I? And who are you?"

He took the letter the next day and I found that from that day, I was no longer getting near the front, just when I wanted to. So I started to get very frustrated being around this Sai Baba.

It would be over fifteen years before I started to understand that he was taking me to the answer.

By the end of the second week, he had passed by me some twenty-eight times. I had about enough of sitting and queuing twice a day for two or more hours each time only to be ignored. Every day I watched groups of people being called by him for an interview. Slowly a feeling of stress started building within. It was time to run away again or get drunk.

I reasoned with myself that maybe I had made a mistake about this person and I was just wasting time by being around him, so I decided to go.

What I really wanted to do was go back to the UK, but I was afraid that anyone who knew me would think that I had somehow failed, that I could not hack it being alone.

I reluctantly decided that I would go down south and in a few weeks maybe catch up with this Sai Baba in Kodaikanal, where I had been told he would normally go in the hottest part of the Indian summer. Once I had made the decision, I got a taxi into Bangalore's main bus station. It was awash with people; think of your worst Christmas shopping then add some more – confusing queues where the people spooned, so that others could not squeeze in. I spent most of the time glaring at the person behind me as he tried to get too close.

"Back, back."

I said it so many times, but the man behind me just looked at me as if I was a little mad. Finally and, with much relief, I got a ticket for the

Why?

next bus going south, which was to the city of Mysore.

On the first morning there I went to a temple on a hill overlooking the city. It would have been very scenic but I had not learned how to see the beauty or spirituality of a place when it seemed to have so few redeeming qualities. There would have been a great view over the city, but I could hardly see it for the blanket of pollution that lay over it. I don't think there was a public toilet, as there was such a strong smell of urine everywhere. It did have its good points; a huge statue of the demon king of Mysore and the design of the temple were quite amazing. The main gate had a high tower over it, which had hundreds of carvings. I didn't go too near to the temple, as the entrance had more beggars than I had seen in my life. I spent a few hours wandering about before making my way back to the city.

I saw some fortunetellers on a street not far from where the bus dropped me off, so I walked back to them hoping that maybe I would find a traditional Indian fortuneteller. I got one that spoke very good English. He asked my name and age and started writing numbers down.

He then told me that so far, this life had been bad for me, but gave plausible reasons as to why, explaining that the worst of my life was over and that later this year I would be forced to have an emotional break from my family. By the time I left him, I felt that I understood many things about my past, leaving me with new hope for my future.

I also asked him where he had learned to do this type of fortunetelling, thinking maybe it had been handed down. He said he had gone on a course in Germany. Not quite as traditional as I was hoping for! I saw a few more sights around the city that afternoon and on returning to my hotel, I considered what I should do next.

After what I had just seen of India from the bus and in three cities, I realised that it was not my idea of a holiday destination. There was nothing more I wanted to see. I could not go back to the UK, so I thought, "Well, I came to see this Sai Baba, I might as well go back there until its time to leave India".

The next morning, I got a bus back to Bangalore, arriving back less than 48 hours from the time I had left. The moment I entered the ashram all the feelings of stress I had when I went away two days before returned, descending like a cloud around my mind. At that, I just thought, ah well, maybe I have not sorted out my life after all. So I stayed on, hoping that maybe something would change, but the next week and a half, Baba continued to ignore me.

I met a medium who volunteered the information that I would get an interview; something that I had not even considered. As a result, I got my hopes up and joined a group of Australians

Why?

around my age, but being ignored continued and I still ended up at the back of the Darshan area.

The following week, another unusual event happened. I had just left the ashram after Darshan and was having a soft drink at a shop across the road. I was sitting in the sun on a plastic garden chair. Around me were the usual beggars and street hawkers trying to make some money from the foreigners, not really the most pleasant of sights. I had just looked up at a nearby tree, when everything changed, becoming amazingly beautiful. A sharpness and perfection I would never have thought possible, individual leaves shone with light that had all the colours of a rainbow. It was so vivid that the tree itself seemed to be painted from the light from a crystal. I was in awe of the beauty of what I was seeing and experiencing.

The experience filled me from within, my mind and body totally relaxed.

Then, as quickly as it had started, it stopped. And I became aware that I was repeating the same word as before,

"Beautiful, beautiful, beautiful".

I don't know how long it lasted for, or how many times I must have said "Beautiful".

After it stopped, I looked around embarrassed in case someone had noticed or heard what I was saying, as I was very aware that there must have been a very stupid expression on my face — a mixture of awe and wonder. But no one

Sai Baba

seemed to have noticed my remarkable experience. I did not understand these two events or even how to express what I had experienced, so again I did not talk about or dwell on either event, but I knew both where somehow triggered by being in the presence of Sai Baba. This fuelled my desire to get his attention even more.

In the beginning of May, Swami usually leaves Whitefield for Kodaikanal, about 12 hours by bus south of Bangalore. This causes some rumours as to the exact timing and some excitement at the prospect of going to another one of Baba's ashrams; this one in the mountains, where it is a lot cooler than Whitefield.

Being ignored by Sai Baba was increasing a feeling of inner turmoil and in about one week I would be leaving for the UK. Still this man had not spoken to me, if anything, he seemed to be going out of his way to turn his back on me each time he neared me in the Darshan area.

On my third day at Kodaikanal, Baba came out as usual; I was sitting in the back again, as he walked by without even seeming to glance in my general direction. Something within me broke and I thought angrily,

"F— you! I don't give a shit about you or this place. I am going to get pissed out of my head".

Then just as angrily, I thought,

"No, I'm not. I'm not gonna get drunk because of you!"

Why?

Right at that moment, I had a small but profoundly shocking revelation about myself. I knew why I had a drink problem. And the only words repeating in my mind then were,

"Sorry, sorry".

I knew that small sentence revealed so much about why I drank.

"I'm not gonna get drunk because of *you*!"

So many things fell into place all at the same time. As I understood what it had taken to get me to this point. I needed to be accepted by people, to be reassured that everything was fine and when I felt that I was not, fear and anxiety would slowly rise. The only way I had of dealing with what I believed others thought of me was to hide in a bottle of alcohol, numb and detached from everything. Drinking allowed me to suppress my feelings for a few days, but then the feelings would start to surface a few days later and I would have to get drunk all over again. And the more I had to deal with people, the more I had to drink.

The more I drank, the more I had days off work and no matter how hard I had tried, I was unable to break this destructive habit.

I was stunned that such a simple thing had caused so much turmoil in my life. Somewhere I had created an emotional point that I could not cross, each time I touched the emotions I would turn away in fear hiding in alcohol. Sai Baba was the hammer that broke through my emotional barrier. I knew my drink problem was gone and I knew all the reasons why it had gone at the very moment I had finished saying the word "*you*".

I did not have any time to dwell on what had happened, as I would be leaving the mountain the next morning for the 24-hour trip back to the UK.

I now knew the reason why I had a drink problem; but there was still a slight fear that once I had one drink I would want another and another, and I would be unable to stop until I was drunk – as I had been doing for so many years before going to India. There was only one way to find out. I would have to go to a pub and have a drink. So three days after leaving India, I was sitting at a bar with a glass of rum in front of me. Looking around the bar, I tried to find things that were different from the last time I was there, but it was all the same. Picking up the glass, I held it up to my eyes, it looked like the same the glass, even felt the same. I sipped at the drink, then held it up to my eyes while swirling the alcohol around my mouth. I felt nothing; I knew the need was gone. Everything I felt about alcohol was different, so I decided to have a few more, just for the hell of it. Well, I had to make sure.

Each time I had one, I knew that I could leave it. I knew beyond a shadow of doubt that the need and compulsion was well and truly gone.

For the rest of that year I went out five or six times, and on each occasion as I drank, I would look at how I

Why?

really felt about it. Did I need the next one? But the old feelings, the compulsion, the need was simply gone. The alcohol's power over my life was simply gone.

That took place in 1992. I still socialize, but I am very happy with a soft drink or a glass of water, occasionally having a wee one.

Not long after returning to England, I met Chris Harris, the medium who had told me about going on the job to Africa. I was with Steve Smith and his girlfriend Nicola (later to become Mrs. Smith). I spoke briefly about India and asked him if we could all get together for a meditation some time. He agreed and to my surprise, we managed to arrange it for one night that week at Nicola's bedsit.

It was just as well that there were only four of us, as it was a bit of a squeeze for us to sit on the floor. I had the idea that we should chant "Om" for a while, which I am pretty sure Steve and Nicola were not to comfortable with judging by the sound they where making. And unfortunately, four people in a small room doesn't sound the same as several hundred chanting it in an ashram, it definitely didn't sound so good. We then sat quietly for a while and had a general conversation about spirituality, which didn't really seem to go anywhere. It did not take long before we had another silence. It kind of marked the end of our little gathering.

As we stood to leave, I started to have a strange experience. My chest had suddenly become very warm, then as it intensified, my whole chest tingled as if I was being gently tickled from within, all I could do was smile. The feeling of happiness within was almost overwhelming. I had felt the warmth several times in India but nothing like this, it was difficult even to speak. Looking at the others I asked,

"Can't yous feel this?"

I felt that I was going to burst with the feeling, but Steve and Nicola just looked at me as if I was strange.

"Can't yous feel this?", I said again.

By now, the experience was at its peak and I was smiling as broadly as the Cheshire Cat from Alice in Wonderland.

The look on there faces was of disbelief and concern, that maybe I had just gone a little mad.

Although Chris had been silent, I had noticed that when I had looked at him he was looking above my head.

"I can see a white light above your head", he said, breaking what was becoming a long silence and taking Steve and Nicola's attention off of me.

"Why don't yous come to my home one day next week?", said Chris.

"Sorry I'm busy all next week", replied Steve.

Nicola would be free the following Thursday and I just smiled and nodded my head, the experience was already fading.

So we made arrangements to meet, then said our goodbyes. By now it was dark and I had to walk about a mile back home. I felt not just happy, but at peace as I went home that night.

We got together about mid-afternoon the following Thursday. The conversation started where we had finished the week before — talking about God, energy and

Why?

the meaning of life, all the questions I've since found have no real answers.

We talked several hours, I could not keep up with Nicola and Chris, so I sat back on the sofa relaxing, just listening as the hours past. M, my mind wondered wandered off, not always keeping track of what was being said. I vaguely remember part of their conversation being about forgiveness and my thoughts went towards my father.

A small smile came to my face.

"I forgive you", I thought.

As I thought this, the centre of my chest started the same tickling sensation that I had experienced the week before, but this time it increased in intensity, then suddenly my whole chest seemed to explode with energy. Years of emotional pain where being ripped away in moments.

My entire body seemed to be on fire, tears were running freely down my face. I desperately wanted to thrust my hands onto the ground, thinking that it would somehow earth the feelings that my body was experiencing, but I was not even capable of getting off my seat.

Within moments of the experience starting, I knew that a forgiveness had happened between my father and I. Over the years, I had started to understand that maybe he was violent because it was passed on from his father, or even his father before him. So what right did I have to do anything other than forgive him? I had in the past often thought,

"I forgive you. What happened doesn't matter".

But these thoughts never seemed enough, they felt empty. This time though, it was different. This time something far deeper had happened; emotions connected with my father were being washed away; I knew that a forgiveness had finally happened. Several hours later I drove home, probably still in a bit of shock and wondering how forgiving my past was going to change my future. However, it would be several years before I understood that forgiving my father would not allow me to escape from why my violent childhood had happened in the first place.

Over the next few months, I woke several times almost drunk on a feeling of bliss, a feeling so tangible that I could exhale it with every breath. There seemed to be no rhyme or reason as to when it happened.

As I wasn't working, I would often walk several miles a day just for something to do. On one of these occasions that I woke to the feelings of euphoria, I walked the three miles to the town centre smiling, as I was experiencing the feeling of bliss within. When I got into the town centre, I headed to one of the shopping malls. As I neared it, I had to make a right turn off the high street to the mall. I turned the corner smiling and my eyes locked with those of a Buddhist monk coming out of the mall; he was perhaps 50 metres away. We looked straight at each other. Smiling, I nodded at him, then for a brief moment I had a strange tingling sensation. The next thing I knew, I was standing inside the mall.

I stopped, stunned, looking around, wondering how the hell I had managed to walk over 50 metres through a

Why?

crowd of people and then into a shopping mall without being aware of any of it.

The feeling of bliss that I had experienced all that morning, evaporated quicker than a morning mist. I looked behind me and there was the old monk looking at me, this time he was smiling. All I could do in return was frown, still smiling; he turned and walked off.

In confusion, I went on into the mall and found a seat. What the hell had just happened? My mind could not comprehend it, so after a while I decided to find the monk, as he somehow caused this strange experience. I spent more than an hour wandering around the town centre, but he had gone.

I later came to understand that what had happened was an answer to something I had thought about often since giving up on the spiritual churches. "How can I help others without getting involved with all the nonsense associated with what so many people referred to as the ego?"

Here was a man going around praying to whatever his concept of God was, creating a positive energy and minding his own business. In that simple act, anyone who came near to him got to share in his positive energy, getting what they needed, but not necessarily what they wanted – as opposed to psychics and healers that try to give what people want rather than what they need.

It took me several years to understand what had happened that day and it was the first time that I had ever reached one of the many states of meditation – something I have not done since.

In meditation you are supposed go beyond the body and the mind. There is an old saying; *If you think you are meditating, you are not – you are only contemplating.*

I spent a lot of time contemplating what had happened in the ashram. While I was there, Baba gave one discourse with a translator; the first thing he said was,

"Prema Swarupa…"

"Embodiments of Love", said the translator.

It was how he always started his talks, indicating that each person was the embodiment of God's love. I thought, well if that is my true reality then anger can't be a part of me.

Over the years I had often been prone to very violent thoughts that seemed to come out of the blue. I would just be walking down a street and anger would well up for no apparent reason; in my mind I would punch someone or would imagine having my hands around someone's throat. I would try to push the thought aside, but even then, I would be left with a deep sadness and self-loathing. This part of my nature caused me to hate myself, as I seemed to have no control over these thoughts at all.

I also remember reading a bit by Doctor John Hislop, a long-time follower of Sai Baba, who had written some very good books and had a lot of attention from Baba.

"You should offer everything to God."

So I decided to put the two thoughts together, each time I had one of these violent thoughts, I would then say to myself,

"Dear God, please accept that thought as an offering to you, as it is not part of my true self."

Why?

At first I did that almost to a point of paranoia every time I had a violent thought.

Almost a year later I was in a cafe with Steve, having a general conversation, when he asked,

"How are your thoughts?"

I frowned, trying to remember the last time that I had a really violent thought and couldn't.

I could only reply,

"Ah yeah, I'm good".

Steve had had no idea what I had been practicing over the last year and as the change had been gradual, I had not even noticed the improvement in the state of my mind.

I then started to pay more attention to my thoughts, noticing how violent thoughts frequently seemed to be accompanied by a perceivable external energy that I would quite literally walk into. It would be a few more years before I came to understand a little bit better that external energy would feed on the feeling that lay hidden within. Even with thoughts, the old saying has a lot of truth – "Like attracts like".

In India, I had often heard people talk about how society creates negative energy through its collective thoughts, until then, I had never considered that some of those momentary violent thoughts that I had had, may have been me touching some of society's more negative thoughts.

It also put into perspective some stories I had read about monks who would walk through a village or town and purify it; their positive thoughts purifying the place of any negative energy the people had created, thus helping the minds of those living there.

Since leaving India, I hadn't been working properly for over almost eight months, in part because I was hoping to move away from carpentry, as I always felt stressed by the work and the conditions of the building sites. Most jobs were like working in a poorly lit cave and my normal working week was between sixty and eighty-four hours, but after eight months with nothing new on the horizon, I ended up going back to carpentry. As I felt better about myself, I also felt better able to deal with the demands of work.

The first job back was fitting out a Chrysalis Records recording studio in London with my brother Liam. I had kept in touch with one of the carpenters from the job in Africa and it was him who effectively got us a place. This was very fortunate, as there was very little work available, as the UK was still in a recession, but this job was paying several pounds more than the normal going rate.

There were several other carpenters that I had known from the job in Africa, although I had never really spoken to them. This job would be much the same, but after several weeks I heard through the guy that got Liam onto the job, that the others I had worked with found it hard to believe the changes in me. It had been almost two years since working in Africa when I had last seen them. They found it hard to believe that someone could change so much in such a short period of time. When he told me that, I thought, "Well yeah, I am much happier now, smiling a lot and a non-drinking

Why?

vegetarian." Quite a different person from the depressed, negative drunk they had met two years before.

Being told that and seeing it so clearly in myself, made me feel more confident about the future.

Unfortunately, we had only been working for a month when the Oriental investors arrived one morning and promptly sacked all the contractors. Not for the lack of quality, but simply because it was costing too much.

Happily, Liam and I got another job straightaway working up north, fitting out a ship.

Again, we were fortunate in that the money was more than the normal going rate. Plus, I was no longer drinking, so almost all of the money I earned was saved, it was only a matter of four months and I had the money to return to India. Over the past year I had become more convinced that Sai Baba had been the catalyst for the changes that had taken place within me and for several months I had a growing feeling that I should go back to India to thank him for what he had done. This time, I felt that I should spend more time at the Ashram. I thought that one week more than last year should be enough, bringing the total time that I would spent in India to six weeks.

Sai Baba

Chapter Five

The Dream

A few days before going, I had a very vivid dream of Prema Sai, Sai Baba's next incarnation.

Baba has said that he is the reincarnation of an Indian Saint by the name of Sai Baba of Shirdi, who died in 1918, predicting that he would return in eight years; Sai Baba was born in 1926. He also announced that there would be a third incarnation called Prema Sai.

I was sitting on the floor opposite a young man that I knew to be Prema Sai. The room we were in was very simple, with white walls and some cushions on the floor; he was just a few feet from me. As I was looking at him, he raised his right hand above his head and looked to his right, indicating a painting on the wall. It was a green lotus surrounded by nine figures in three sets of three, forming an inverted triangle around the lotus. As I looked at it, every part of my being knew that what he was showing me represented 'completion'.

I woke from the dream and thought about what I had seen of Prema Sai. At first I was amazed at how beautiful he was. When I was looking at him a part of me knew that what I was looking at was a person that had a perfect balance between male and female.

Why?

Several years later I was reading the *Ram Katha Vahini*, a book that Baba himself wrote. In it, Baba was describing Rama and how perfect his form was. It was also a perfect description of how Prema Sai will look.

I had some ideas as to the meaning of the dream; the green lotus was the same colour that is depicted by the Hindu and Buddhist traditions as the heart chakra. As for the feeling I had about something being complete, I hoped that was me, but in just a few weeks I would know that to be wrong.

I was at that time making the final arrangements for a return trip to India. I figured that baba would be in Kodaikanal, so I would fly into New Delhi then get an internal flight down south to Madurai, then a bus up the mountain to Kodai. The cheapest flight I could find was with Aeroflot, the Russian airline. A decision I would come to regret, but eventually be thankful for.

When I walked onto the airplane, I was surprised at the smell of stale cigarette smoke and the cabin was darker than normal, obviously from years of staining from the cigarette smoke. As I sat, I thought that the carpet moved slightly, puzzled I looked down and using my feet I found the carpet moved freely backwards and forwards. Intrigued, I looked more closely, it was only a long narrow strip that was fraying at the edges and ran under several seats in front and back of my seat.

As I was still looking down, I heard an announcement,

"Its international law, we have to give you safety instructions".

The Dream

It sounded like a reluctant apology that they had to do it.

There were still lots of people putting bags in the overhead lockers, while others where standing in the aisle, talking during the safety instructions. I could only look on in disbelief; no one seemed to pay any attention to the cabin crew.

Maybe I was a little too aware by the time we started to take off, that I was not in the newest of aeroplanes and judging by the inside of the cabin, an aeroplane that was perhaps not that well maintained.

As we started up the runway and the engines started to roar for take off, I was aware of every creak and groan of the cabin and this one made lots. The whole aeroplane seemed to protest at the stresses of take off. Fortunately, within a few minutes we were above the clouds and the aeroplane seemed to relax. It took me a little bit longer.

The flight itself was uneventful, other than the vegetarian food. A portion of slightly burnt peas, with what looked like a hash brown, but wasn't. I knew I was going to get hungry over the next 18 hours.

On every flight I had been on, prior to landing, the crew would always inform people not to stand up or get things out of the overhead lockers. Unfortunately, most of the passengers on this flight, had obviously never heard this warning. As the aeroplane was in a steep descent, many people stood up and started to rifle through the overhead lockers. This was definitely the most interesting flight I had ever been on! And after the take off in London, I was very aware of the noises the plain might

Why?

make as we started the descent into Moscow, but the landing was one of the smoothest I had ever had. Afterwards, I wondered if the pilot was also aware that if he landed too hard, that maybe some of this old plane might not make if to the end off the runway!

The second leg of the journey was much the same as the first, although longer. Eventually, I arrived tired and hungry in New Delhi early in morning, but still eager to get to my destination as quickly as possible.

On exiting the plain it was like being hit with a wall of heat and smells. I knew that at this time of the year, Sai Baba would be in the mountains at Kodaikanal, a much cooler place than New Delhi. I didn't want to hang around in this heat, even for a day.

I got a bus straight over to the domestic airport. The short trip was both amazing and shocking; to see so much poverty and wealth side by side, the smells of incense and pollution everywhere. Even though it was still early morning, the place buzzed with hundreds of people. Whenever the bus stopped, trinkets or food were pushed through the window. Smiling children, often with no more clothes than a pair of shorts, would stretch out their arms, shouting "Pen, pen, pen".

On arriving at the airport, I made my way to the Air India sales desk.

"How can I help you sir?" asked a young lady.

"I would like the next flight to Madurai please."

She tapped the information into her computer and after a few moments looked up.

"There is no direct route today sir, you will have to take two flights."

"How much will that cost?"

The Dream

The cost was more than double last years flight, putting it way over what I had set aside for internal flights.

"Is there anything cheaper?"

"No sir, the nearest city with a direct flight would be Madras. From there you could take the train to Madurai."

"Where is Madras?" I asked.

She pulled out a small map of India from under her desk and pointed with a pen to a place on the East coast.

"It's just a short journey from there to Madurai."

Maybe it was because I was so tired and desperate to get to Kodaikanal, that I did not stop to think that a small map of India did not mean a small journey. The UK can fit into India twelve times, so to get a real perspective, I would have needed to get a map twelve times larger than the one I was looking at.

I did not want to wait, so I decided on a flight to Madras, unaware that it could take me almost 12 hours by train to Madurai, then another four hours up the mountain to Kodaikanal itself. I ended up having an overnight stay in Madras, then another in Madurai. The journey to Kodaikanal managed to stretch on for two days. No matter how fast I tried to get there, I was slowed down waiting for planes, trains and buses. Hanging about in strange parts of India wasn't as bad as I thought. Having had two good nights before the final four-hour bus trip up the 7,000 feet to Kodaikanal Hill station, I arrived mentally worn out, but physically refreshed.

It was almost exactly a year to the day since I had left Kodaikanal. I found that Sai Baba was giving all the overseas people priority seating. So I was near or in the front row almost every Darshan (twice a day).

I had been wondering about this strange Hindu custom of touching Baba's feet; many people had said that

Why?

it was special. Supposedly the body of a true holy man is full of positive energy, or so I was told. So the theory is, if I were to touch him I would take on some of that pure positive energy. Hearing this, I thought that I would at least try to touch his feet — just out of curiosity.

After a few days, the opportunity came along, so being very careful not to trip him, I reached out as he walked past. It was like being punched with energy in the centre of my chest, leaving me on a happy high for several hours. It was definitely more than positive energy and I wanted some more. So whenever the opportunity came along to touch Baba I took it. It would always leave me with a deep happiness, but by that evening or the following day I would return to normal and that made 'normal' very difficult.

The more this happened to me, the more confused I became and the more I doubted the need for such experiences.

I was also having lots of dreams about Baba that I could not understand, so I ended up asking almost anyone that would listen what they thought the meaning might be, but any answers they could give only led to even more questions. So instead of understanding what was going on, I became more and more confused.

Over the years I had come to notice that at the end of every answer there was always another question, so anything that left me with questions was not the answer I was looking for. What was the point of these experiences? If I touched his feet I was up, only to come back

The Dream

down. If I had a dream again, I thought I had to understand it, only ending up being more confused.

After two-three weeks of this, I had become really pissed off. I could do without the intensity of these ups and downs and the running around chasing the meaning of the dreams. What had been happening was becoming too much to bear. It was not an experience that I needed, it was a balance within that I wanted and so I decided to write a letter to Baba asking for the experiences to stop.

I took the letter to Darshan, stretching out my arm as he walked past, but he did not even look at it. Sitting in a cafe afterwards, I put the letter in a bin, relieved that Baba had not taken it. The truth is, I knew I did not want to give up even a small amount of bliss or the vivid dreams I had been having, even if it did cause confusion.

But though he never took the letter, straight away there was a change; the chances to touch Baba stopped, and with that, the ups and downs as well, as did the vivid dreams. I started feel a balance that had been missing from my life for a long time.

I did manage to understand some more of the Prema Sai dream. I had met an older Indian couple, who explained that each Avatar has three aspects: Brahma, Vishnu and Shiva — the Creator, the Preserver and the Destroyer. Now I understood that three sets of the three figures around the lotus represented the three parts of the Sai trinity: Shirdi Baba, Sathya Sai Baba, and Prema Sai, each incarnation having three aspects of divinity.

Why?

The last piece for me to understand was the green lotus. There was a Hindu New Year celebration when I was at Kodai. The Darshan area was decorated with bunting and lots of painted lotuses, each a different colour and within each petal, a symbol representing one of the major religions.

As I walked into the Darshan area, the first one I saw was green. Immediately I knew the significance of what I had seen in the dream and what I was seeing in the Darshan area.

The green lotus in the dream had no religious symbols in any of its petals, but all of these in the Darshan area did. I knew that what he had shown me in the dream was, 'This is the love of God without religion', referring to the time when Prema Sai would be a young man.

While in Kodaikanal, Easter came and went with no celebrations to mark it. It caused me to remember the church celebrations as a child, being sent to church and having to kiss the feet of Jesus. As I knelt near the altar awaiting my turn, I would watch all the other people kissing the statue. The priest would give it a quick wipe before moving on to the next person, I did not like the idea that I would have to kiss after all of them, but I had no choice. It had to be done and done quickly, and afterwards without anyone noticing, I would quickly wipe my lips on my clothes. The memory made me smile, but it kept returning to annoy me over the next several months, eventually becoming part of something quite magical.

The Dream

By the beginning of May, Baba had moved back to Brindavan and I had moved back into the ashram accommodation there.

The Darshan area had been changed. The tree was gone and in its place stood a large green and white hall, which was very hot. It soon became known as Baba's greenhouse because of how it trapped the heat. The other disadvantage to the hall was that it had been broken down into blocks; the students from Baba's College were sitting in the first two blocks, then in the block behind them were the teachers, doctors, VIPs; then the general public took up the next four blocks.

Although I had had so many opportunities to touch Baba's feet, he had never looked at me since I had arrived in India. So there was an undercurrent of emotion that I was beginning to feel more and more; he was still ignoring me just like last year. Every day, I watched him talk to people and take several groups for interviews. It made me want to leave, but again I couldn't; I had to stay. I could not go back to the UK and I did not want to travel in India. Fortunately, there were only three weeks left and I was on a countdown, but with each passing day, the ashram began to feel more and more like a prison.

My fear of having to stay was heightened by some stories I heard of Baba telling people not to leave. Then I met one lady whose passport Swami had taken, saying to her,

"Don't leave, stay here".

(She told me when I met her on another trip that Baba had given the passport back.)

Why?

So, just in case, I stopped taking my flight tickets and passport into the Darshan area. Up until that point, I thought that keeping them with me was the safest thing to do, but the thought of being told to stay was more frightening than losing them. I had got to the point that there was no way I was staying one minute longer in India than I needed to.

Baba took to walking through the men and students in the front blocks, and only at the weekend when there was an overspill from the hall, would he venture to the back where I would be, so I decided to try and sit in the VIP block. Luckily, before coming to India I had bought some quality white trousers and white shirts and at least I looked the part.

Doctors, teachers and the VIPs waited in a separate area to get into the Darshan hall. So with only slight apprehension I joined them, trying to look, as best as I could, that I belonged there.

On the first day, I was so nervous that I found myself looking around for some sign that what I was about to do was fine. On looking up in to the sky I could see several eagles. I thought, "That's a good sign, I am meant to do this". And I took some comfort in that thought. Sure enough, as I got to the Seva Dals (the ashram volunteers) who check who is who, I was let straight in.

This went on for several days and even though I sat in the middle of the block, it was better than the uncertainty of having to wait for an hour in the token lines, never sure of how far away I was going to be from Baba.

The Dream

Foolishly, before each Darshan I would look into the sky for eagles and sure enough they would be there, so I felt that what I was doing was alright.

One morning, there were perhaps a dozen eagles gliding on the thermals high overhead. Again, I took it as a good sign as I moved closer to the Seva Dals, but this time they stopped me. There was a Seva Dal on either side of me, and several more in front. Although they didn't say anything, it was obvious they wanted me to explain who I was and why I was in the VIP line. I couldn't think of anything to say and they just continued to stare, the seconds became excruciatingly long and I could feel a nervousness rising through the body. My heart was pounding loudly in my ears and then my body began to shake noticeably. Even my chin knotted up and my lower lip was trembling, I was trying my hardest not to burst into tears.

My body had betrayed me, I was a child again — scared of being punished, the adults staring, expecting an explanation and I had none. There was nothing I could do, but the fear of having been found out was disproportionate to what was happening; this was something from my past.

I became aware of one of the Seva Dals waving his hand for me to go through and somehow I managed to get one leg in front of the other. By the time I sat down in the hall, the shaking had reduced to a mild trembling with a feeling of rawness throughout the body. By the end of Darshan, I was already trying to bury what had happened. I couldn't and wouldn't think too much

Why?

about it, it was simply too embarrassing; although my reaction stayed at the back of my mind.

I knew I would never try to sit up front again; I would sit in the token lines from now on and I hoped that no one I knew had seen my irrational fear.

I also couldn't believe how foolish I had been to look for signs that what I was doing was right, instead of just making a decision and getting on with it.

Then rumours started spreading that the foreigners in the ashram accommodation were going to be moved out to make way for the students' parents who would be coming to the ashram for a yearly event called 'Summer Showers' (Baba would give discourses on Indian culture to the students of the Sathya Sai Baba College, their parents and some guests). Sure enough, all the people in the accommodation where asked to leave. This dragged up feelings within me of not being good enough and added to my desire to get back to the UK.

During the event, Darshan almost stopped, as in the morning, Baba would be driven out in a car, get out where the crowd had been waiting for several hours, wave, get back in and drive off to a lecture hall to give a discourse on Indian culture to the students. This went on for 10 days.

One day in particular, I had been standing outside the lecture hall in the rain listening to Baba's discourses, being envious of those inside with him. The feelings I was having reminded me of that traumatic event from my childhood when I woke up one day to find that my sister and my brothers had been taken out for the day

The Dream

by my father. I had deliberately been left behind—excluded.

It caused me a great deal of pain to be rejected and here I was almost 25 years later, standing outside a building remembering those feelings all over again.

I pushed the feelings aside and was a bit confused by them as I wondered, "If I've forgiven my father, why is there still pain left from my memories of my childhood?"

I did the only thing I could think of, I offered the pain to God and tried to ignore it.

In the afternoons Baba also gave discourses to the general public. There was a translator, but because of the poor sound quality of the PA system and the translator's accent, I could not understand what was said. It only added a few more painful hours sitting crossed legged.

Chapter Six

A Matter of Trust

All interaction with Baba had stopped since the letter I wrote in Kodaikanal and my feelings that my stay was little more than a self-imposed prison sentence were increasing by the day, but fortunately I was about to be released.

Five days before I was due to leave, I gave my flight tickets to an agent to have them reconfirmed. Aeroflot had advised that this should be done 72 hours before the flight's departure. The next day, the agent was at the gates of the ashram, so I asked how he was getting on with my ticket. He told me that there was no Aeroflot office in Bangalore and that he would have to send a fax to New Delhi at an extra cost of 50 rupees. Of course I said, "Yes", and left him to it.

By this time, I was feeling quite happy saying to people, "At last, my prison sentence is almost over'. I had had enough of Baba seeming to go out of his way to ignore me; so on the final day of my trip, I was very relieved and happy to be going. On my last day, a friend decided that if he sat next to me, Baba would walk close to us, as he expected Baba to give me some attention, since it would be my last Darshan.

Why?

This I thought very unlikely, as for the past four of the six weeks, I had seen more of Swami's back than anything else. I was not to be disappointed, but my friend was, as Swami came nowhere near us. I was just relieved that the whole trip was finally over.

After Darshan, I went to the agent's office with two friends to pick up my ticket. On arriving, I was handed a fax, which said, 'Please inform Mr. Hempsey that he has not reconfirmed his flight within the 72 hours that we advised, so we have given his seat to another passenger. Please ask him to reconfirm on another flight'.

The only thing I could do was stare unbelievingly at the offending piece of paper in my hand in a numb silence. After a few minutes, I handed it to one of my friends without saying anything to him. After a few moments, I thought I would have to pick them off the floor, as they where laughing so much. I thought, "It's OK, I have enough money, so there's no real problem, and I don't have to be back in the UK for anything", so when they had stopped laughing, I asked the agents to get me the next flight out of India, hoping it would only take a few days at the most.

The agents tried to get a confirmed flight, but all they could manage to get was a waiting list and even then, only part of the journey – New Delhi to Moscow, but not Moscow to London; or Moscow to London, but not Delhi to Moscow. Even if I could get to Moscow, I was told that it would cost me $100 a night for accommodation. With an undetermined stay there, it seemed beyond my financial ability; for two nights in Moscow I could live for a month in India.

Word quickly spread around the ashram that I had missed my flight. I had to show a lot of self-restraint, as strangers would come up to me telling me how lucky I was to be staying, "Baba wants you here". Fortunately, the Australians just laughed, which was much more bearable.

After a few days, I was told that there was in fact an office in Bangalore for Aeroflot. If only the agent had taken my ticket there in the first place, I would now be sitting in the UK, a much happier person — or so I thought!

I informed the agents that there was an Aeroflot office in Bangalore and asked for my ticket; this part I would do myself. They were good enough to offer me transport into the city centre, on the back of a scooter. This in itself was an adventure, as there seem to be no rules for driving in India — just use your horn every few seconds, pull out whenever you can (even when there's another vehicle bearing down on you), and have a sixth sense for the madness of other drivers. It seems to work for the Indians.

Luckily, I arrived at the offices unscathed and it only took me a few moments to pry my fingers from the back of the scooter. It was good fun, but not something I would like to do every day. It's not just cats that have nine lives, but Indian drivers as well. And, since I wasn't Indian, I wasn't about to push my luck.

I entered the offices and approached the inquiries desk, and with a smile said,

Why?

"Hi, through no fault of mine, I've managed to miss my flight to London, and I was hoping you could get me on the next available flight out of the country".

The man behind the desk spoke English with a strong Indian accent and wobbled his head as he spoke.

"I'm afraid this is not possible Sir, as Aeroflot is giving 25 per cent off all flights out of India, so they are fully booked for some time."

"You have to", I pleaded.

"I have to leave the country!!"

More than little bit of desperation had slipped into my voice.

"The only thing I can do, Sir, is put your name on the waiting lists."

"But my visa is running out soon."

(There were only four-and-a-half months left on it.)

"There is still nothing I can do, Sir".

"Well, can you change the carrier?"

That actually brought a big smile to his face.

"No other airline will touch this ticket, as you have purchased the cheapest one on the market; you'd be better trying to buy a new one."

"And how much would that be?", I asked.

After some playing about with his computer, he told me in Indian rupees, then converted it to English pounds. It would cost me about 20 pound less than I had paid for the return ticket.

"No thanks", I said.

He then set about putting my name on several flight waiting lists and informed me that I should check again tomorrow.

On leaving the building, I thought, "There's two ways to deal with this, get angry and shout at people, which in India is a total waste of time, or quietly resign myself to the inevitable, with the option to do as much as possible to get out of this bloody country". I took the second choice.

About a week into this, I got a front row in Darshan and as Swami was walking past me I was shouting in my head, "When am I going to leave this place?"

At that, Swami stopped in front of the person next to me and asked someone a few rows back,

"When are you leaving?"

"On the 25th, Swami", came the reply.

To which Baba said,

"Ah 50th, very happy".

Then he walked away.

My mind somehow managed to jump; "Double 25th and you've got 50th. There's no way that I'm bloody well doubling my stay from six to twelve weeks" — so I started to redouble my efforts to get out of the country.

Still, all I was managing to get was wait listed, Moscow to London or Delhi to Moscow with an unknown length of stay in Moscow. After another week of trying, I gave up and accepted the inevitable.

This had now been going on for almost two weeks and had brought much delight to many people around the ashram. They thought it was a wonderful game Baba was playing with me and wasn't I so lucky. Hell I didn't think so.

Baba was about to go to Puttaparthi, so I gave in. I had had enough. For the last time I went to the Banga-

Why?

lore office with the intention of doubling my original stay.

I sat expectantly behind a table I had come to know so well, asking, "Is there a flight on 29th June?" The man on the other side of the table went into his computer and after a moment, said with a head wobble,

"Yes".

"Can you book and confirm it for me?"

"No", he replied, "Wait list."

So even four weeks before the departure date, all I could do was get my name on a waiting list. I would have to try and re-confirm at a closer date to the flight.

Before I finally gave in, I had noticed that I kept thinking,

"I believe in you, but I don't trust you".

I had been saying it to myself for some time, repeating it almost like a mantra before I actually started to consider,

"Why don't I trust you?"

He had given me no reason to distrust him and every reason to trust him. So I decided to change what I was thinking to,

"Why, why don't I trust you?"

I got the answer a few days later and it was not what I expected.

On the 3rd of June, Baba went to Puttaparthi. I arrived at the ashram several hours after him. The ashram was like a small town. Whitefield and Kodaikanal ashrams could easily fit into it several times over.

When I arrived, Baba was already walking around a large group of people, so I went to the Darshan area.

The moment I saw him, the memories and emotions of when I was about 11 or 12 years old came flooding back, bringing me to tears, which I then tried to hide.

At that time of my life, I had been praying to God each night, crying myself to sleep, hoping he would take me away from the pain of the life I was in. But I never seemed to get an answer and the pain and loneliness didn't stop.

Eventually I gave up praying. It was then I stopped trusting in God. I had occasionally thought of that time and dismissed it as something that I did not really mean, or as just the outpourings of a lonely child looking for affection.

But 20 years on, I was re-experiencing the way I had felt as that child. This time though, the pain was being released and I came to an understanding that it was then as a child, that I had stopped trusting in the divine to take away my pain.

That same day, I started to become ill with flu-like symptoms and a nose that felt as if it was running a marathon. By the following morning, I was wondering, "How can one head have so much mucous?" But regardless of how I was feeling, I was still going to have my morning cigarette and cup of tea in a shop outside the ashram.

I had already been awake for several hours, so I was looking forward to my first cigarette of the day. To my surprise and disappointment, I couldn't taste it at all. Regardless of how deeply I inhaled and held all that nicotine in my lungs, I felt and tasted nothing. There was another man in the cafe smoking, he had left his

Why?

packet on the table and I could see that his brand of cigarettes was far stronger than the brand I normally smoked, so not to be put off, I asked him for one.

I sparked up and took another deep breath. Even then, no matter how deeply I inhaled, or how long I held the smoke in my lungs, I still could not taste it or get that usual first nicotine 'high' that I was so used to and seemed need in the morning.

At that time, I had given up trying to stop smoking. The addiction was stronger than I was. I had tried so many times, that I had started to tell others that I had given up trying to give up and accepted that I was well and truly addicted. I didn't care. I had decided that I was at least going to try and live with my addiction.

I went back to the ashram with a pack of tissues, thinking that when the flu was over, I'd have another cigarette. Three days later, something unusual happened. I went to the toilet and as I was passing urine, a stench of nicotine came from it. The smell was so strong that I had to lean backwards choking, waving my hand in front of my face to try and get the stench away.

I didn't know it then but my addiction was gone. At that point I just felt no need or want for a cigarette and as the days and weeks passed, I realised that everything about the addiction was gone. There was none of the usual withdrawal symptoms that I'd had when I had tried to give up before: shortness of breath, tingling in my hands and feet and around my face, being irritable and impatient. None of that happened, it seemed that somehow the nicotine had been removed from the body.

Even having someone blow smoke in my face had no effect, I could breathe it in deeply and it had no effect at all, It simply felt that I had never smoked in my life.

It was roughly two months since Kodaikanal. I had become increasingly bothered by the memory of not wanting to kiss the statue of Jesus; it was like a mild itch that I couldn't quite scratch.

So, I thought to make up for my past, I would, if I got the opportunity, kiss Baba's feet instead. The chances of doing this were not easy, he would have to be standing in front of me and I would also have to ask him. Speaking out was not one of my strong points. Sure enough, whenever Baba came near I became apprehensive, my stomach started to churn and I was unable to speak.

Then one very strange day it happened. I got a good token and managed a front row, sitting opposite the ladies, looking towards the Poornachandra Hall. At around three o'clock, Baba came out walking through the ladies. Instead of going straight, he turned left at the end of the ladies' area, then across the front of the main gates to some little shelters that the teachers would sit in.

It looked as if he was just going to take some letters, when he surprisingly stepped into one of the shelters. Immediately it started to rain but it was not normal, it was as though someone had just thrown buckets of water from only a few feet above the ground, the droplets were over a foot long and caught the air, forming half bubbles before slashing onto the ground. My jaw dropped in astonishment as I looked at these huge

Why?

drops of rain bouncing on the ground. As I looked up at this marvel, I could also see that outside the Darshan area just beyond the Poornachandra Hall, that it was raining normally there. It was so distinct and heavy that it looked almost like a wall of water. People behind me had started clapping.

Then very quickly, Baba stepped out of the alcove and it all stopped. He was only about 15 feet from me and moving much faster than normal, so he would be past me in moments.

I blurted out.

"Baba, can I kiss your feet?"

By then he was about six feet out and straight in front of me. He immediately took a left turn and within a few strides was standing in front of me.

As he neared I couldn't see his feet because of his robe but at the last moment it fell back. I bent forward and kissed his foot. As I began to sit up, my mind was so clear and empty, but before I had sat up completely a thought entered my head.

"Did anyone see me?"

And at the same time, I almost looked around to see if anyone had seen me what I had just done.

The moment I had finished the thought I just felt such dismay.

Was this the real reason for wanting to kiss his feet? A bit of show, to say to others,

"Look what I've done"?

I left Darshan feeling ashamed. It was over two years before I spoke to anyone about the rain or how my ego had been so easily deflated with a simple thought.

Two weeks into being in Puttaparthi, I eventually got my confirmation to leave. The rest of my stay was still difficult, watching as each day Swami would take people for interviews. The best view that I was getting of him was still of his back. Finally, my last day had arrived and of course, I was glad to be going.

Again, my friend Raj was convinced that the reason Swami had not given me any attention six weeks earlier was that he knew that I would be staying, so today would be different. Raj ended up more upset than I was when Swami gave me a very wide berth.

I arrived at Bangalore Airport to find that my domestic flight had been delayed, but I was assured that I would still be on time for my international flight. Someone would meet me at the domestic airport and help get my bags, then take me across the runway to the international terminal. This would cut out the need for a taxi and also cut out all the traffic; getting me to the domestic terminal in minutes instead of up to an hour.

When my flight landed I went to the information desk to find the person who would be helping me, but no one new what I was talking about and the only answer that I could get from staff was, "What can I do?"

This reply was accompanied by a shrug of the shoulders and the customary Indian head wobble.

I waited nervously. My bags seemed to take forever and of course they were about the last ones out. As soon as I got them I rushed out of the terminal to a taxi, I thrust more money at the driver than was needed and said,

Why?

"Get me to the international airport as quickly as possible".

The driver smiled at the money and shook his head with what I took to be a yes. As the taxi left the domestic airport, there was a ramp leading onto the Indian equivalent of a dual carriageway. The moment we left the ramp I expected him to accelerate, only to find that the only way this car could go faster was down hill, preferably with a strong wind. The car actually slowed down as we entered the dual carriageway. I leaned forward in my seat and said,

"Faster, faster!"

The driver turned to me, and with a smile and a wobble of his head, said,

"We are going as fast as we can, Sir".

All I could do was sit back and watch as several taxis shot past me on the way to the other terminal. Eventually, the taxi lumbered into the international airport. I thought, "Maybe there is still a chance". It was 12 o'clock the exact time my flight was due to take off. Maybe it would be delayed, so I tried to rush into the terminal, but was stopped by the police asking to see my ticket. I showed it to them.

One started to laugh and then said something in his own language to the other officers, who also started to have a good laugh. They all knew that my flight had taken off on time. Well, at least someone thought it funny. I still rushed to the Aeroflot desk, only to be told that it had left on time. There was nothing they could do about another flight. I would have to go to their offices in the city, which would not be open until ten the next morning.

I tried to get angry at Baba as I felt that he was the reason for me being in India, but I couldn't. I did manage half-heartedly to call him some names that I think would not be found even in a dictionary. Still, I am sure he would not mind, because if he was like every one else, he was probably having a good laugh.

I thought, "I was not stranded, just delayed". The only thing I could think of doing was to go and have a cup of tea. There was a machine in one corner with some seats; I sat down for some time feeling strangely very peaceful. Part of me expected to panic, given that the last time I missed the flight it took six weeks to get another one, instead everything felt Just OK.

I had been sitting for a few minutes, when a young couple came over to the tea machine.

"Hi", said the young man.

I nodded back with a smile.

"You going home?"

"Nope, my flight from Bangalore was delayed, so I missed the international flight".

"What are you going to do?"

"I haven't got to that bit yet. In the morning though, I have to go to Connaught Place to see if I can get a flight."

I explained part of what had been going on, and we all had a laugh. They gave me the address of the hotel they had come from which happened to be near to Connaught Place and was inexpensive, so all I needed was a taxi and I didn't really care how fast it could go.

Why?

At 10 o'clock, I turned up at the Aeroflot office hoping that I could get a flight within the next few days, only to be told again,

"I can get you on a flight tomorrow from Delhi to Moscow but not Moscow to London. You will have to return tomorrow morning to see if there is any space on the connecting flight."

Resigned to my fate I left the offices thinking,

"God, not this again".

"Was I going to be here for another six weeks?"

Oddly, I still felt relaxed about it.

To keep my mind busy, I walked around the many bazaars in Connaught Place, spending most of the day trying to avoid the many shop owners — if given even a glance, they would try to get me into their shop. The only way to deal with it was to pretend indifference and just keep walking.

The following morning, I returned to the Aeroflot office hoping for some good news. I had arrived early, the offices would not be open till 10 a.m. and it was now just before 9:30. Again, to distract myself, I took a walk around the block, returning just as they opened. I sat down opposite one of their staff and trying not to look or sound desperate, I asked as casually as I could about my connecting flight. A sound I had become so familiar with then ensued, as fingers tapped on the computer keyboard accompanied by the background sound of cars and rickshaws beeping their horns. He didn't even glance up as he unexpectedly said,

"Yes, it's all confirmed, you'll be leaving tonight for London."

I hadn't realised it, but I had been holding my breath. Releasing it I smiled,

"Thank you".

My happiness was only slightly tempered by the fact that I wasn't yet on the airplane, but this time I had nothing to worry about. I caught the flight that night and was impressed as well. Aeroflot had managed to get some new aeroplanes from somewhere. It was great; the changes they had made in only 12 weeks.

Afterwards, I had time to reflect on some of the things that had happened. I understood that I had a deep fear of being alone and stranded in a strange place. A fear of the unknown, which all led me to be very rigid in how I planned anything. I had to get to a place as quickly as possible, with no unexpected changes and my return had to be the same; my need to do it like this was based on fear.

It seemed that the only way to get over something like that, is just to go through it and to deal with it. It wasn't so bad, and I am sure that if it ever happened again I would just trust that it's going to be OK in the end and hope the end is not too far away.

It was July when I got home and my money was running very short again. Within two weeks, I started on a job with my brothers Liam and Mick, fitting out part of a new air traffic control centre just outside of Southampton. It was a nice little job, about 20 minutes away from where I was living and as I did not smoke or drink any more, I managed to save a little each week. After the stresses of India, life just seemed better. I could

Why?

feel how I had been changed and as the month rolled on, my hunger for being in the ashram increased.

By January, I decided that I would go back for Shivaratri (Lord Shiva's night). And after what had happened the last time, I thought that I should go for three months just in case I found myself somehow being forced to stay longer.

I mentioned to my landlady that I would be going and asked if it would be possible to give her my rent on my return, as we had known each other for several years, but she said "No".

I knew that if I was to pay three month's rent up front, I would not be able to afford to go for much more than three weeks. So I had a choice between the room in a house or the chance for change in my life. It did not take long to choose.

So I decided to sell all of my things, as I had nowhere to put them. I did not have very much, except for a very comfortable double pine bed and some nice pictures. I sold some and gave the others away.

Steve Smith asked if he could come along, as I had travelled there several times. I asked him to arrange the flight as he had time off work and could do it more easily than I.

As my travel date neared, I realised that I would still not have enough money to go for three months, even after selling everything, but I felt that the length of time I had decided to go for was right.

Just as I gave Steve the money for the flight, I decided that I had better sort out my tax returns. I had put it off for the past two years, because I thought that I owed money to the taxman. So I sorted out all my receipts, some jobs I had paid tax on and others I had not. I took them to my accountant the day before I was due to go.

He started to work out my returns in front of me and to my surprise, he told me that for the first year, I would get around six hundred pounds back and for the second year I would get about eight hundred pounds back.

I was so surprised that I said,

"What?"

At that, the accountant looked up from his paperwork with a frown and said,

"Were you expecting more?"

Embarrassed, I replied,

"Well no, I expected to owe the taxman some money". He then told me that he would probably have all the returns done by the time I returned to the UK in three months.

So I went with Steve to India. He would be staying for two weeks, and for those two weeks I had a great time. I was completely convinced that Sai Baba's presence was a catalyst for change in my life, but I thought, "My main addictions were gone, what could he possibly do now?"

I was having a pleasant time so far. Unfortunately Steve was not. He was concerned about his girlfriend and his business, so his thoughts were often back in the UK.

I had spoken with an American who had been living in the ashram long-term and he convinced me that I should extend my stay, as I would have

Why?

money on my return to the UK. So I decided to stay for six months.

It was not until Steve had just gone, that my little romance with the ashram ended.

I was sitting in Darshan and Baba had just walked past, when I realised that he probably would not be giving me an interview and the thought of staying here and going to Darshan day in, day out, without any attention for the next five months, almost made me physically sick.

The two previous visits had taught me not to expect too much from Baba, as when I did, disappointment soon followed. So I decided that the only way to manage was to live one day at a time, expect nothing and hope for the best.

Fortunately, each day I went to Darshan, I would feel a gentle, warm, almost swirling feeling in the centre of my chest. It was such a strange feeling, that if anyone asked me if I felt or experienced anything, I would say, no; I found it almost impossible to describe what was happening.

This sensation went on until Shivaratri at the beginning of March. In the Hindu calendar, this festival is a time when the moon is at its weakest point of the entire year. The mind is linked with the moon, so on this night, if you spend it thinking of God, it supposedly allows you to become free of the bad qualities of the mind.

On the morning of Shivaratri, Baba came out wearing a yellow robe.

As he walked into the Darshan area, I became aware of something that started to happen inside me. It was like watching two things at the same time, one inside me and Baba walking around outside. In the inner view, I could see something that looked like a dark cloud, which had the consistency of jelly. I watched, layers of it started to be cut away.

As each layer was cut, I watched as it rose up from my lower chest to the top of my head causing a tingling sensation in the mind as it left the body. The experience continued for most of the Darshan, which lasted for almost two hours.

For the next few days, I had a very sensitive lower back and my head felt equally sensitive; but not quite a headache. Three days later, I had diarrhea, which was jet black. It would seem that something was cleansed from within, on what seemed like several different levels. I have often wondered if it had something to do with the years of alcohol abuse and smoking.

Over the next few months, Baba seemed to be ignoring me. Every so often, I would get a momentary look, but nothing that filled my feeling of emptiness, or that took away the feeling that he was going out of his way to ignore me.

I was also unknowingly starting to suffer from dehydration. It came on slowly over several weeks, as I mistakenly thought I had been drinking enough water. It left me feeling dull; more miserable than was normal (I could be more miserable than most) and often very tired; all of which I put down to being ignored by Baba and being generally unhappy with life.

Why?

Watching people getting interviews every day and wondering what was so wrong with me was not helping my happiness. What had I done that was so bad?

On the two previous visits, some mediums had (unasked for) told me,

"I see you getting an interview".

To say the least, I was disappointed, but this time I walked straight into another one. I had seen an astrologer who had said that on the 23rd of this month, it would be a very auspicious alignment of some planets, and it would affect me because of where it was happening in my natal chart.

So I got my hopes up as I waited for the auspicious alignment to happen. On the morning of the 23rd, Baba called a group of Australians for an interview, most of whom I had become friendly with over the past few weeks and some I had met on previous trips. Of all the days that Baba could have taken these people for an interview, he chose this one to take in almost all of the people I had become friendly with. I had become so used to being let down in my life, that I had already started to bury how I felt, the moment they started to go in for the interview.

Some of them came up to me afterwards, knowing that I had expected something to happen that day. I shrugged it off and smiled as if nothing had happened, denying how I really felt even to myself and trying to carry on as if nothing had happened.

Chapter Six

Cooling Fire

Baba spent one month at Whitefield before going to Kodaikanal. It was about ten days before going to Kodai that I really started to realise that there was something wrong with me. My body was just not working the way it should. I was feeling dull and lethargic all the time. Everything from going to the bathroom to going to sleep just wasn't happening. I explained the symptoms to some friends, who said it was probably dehydration. I though it couldn't be, as I was drinking what I thought was lots of fluids (tea and cola).

The trip to Kodai was much easier this time, as I took a sleeper train, which left Bangalore at 9 o'clock at night and arrived at around 6 o'clock in the morning at Kodai Junction. From there it was a four-hour bus trip up the mountain to Kodaikanal Hill station. I arrived at around 12 o'clock, which left plenty of time to find some accommodation. I rented a little room in an India family's home, about a 20-minute walk from Swami's house. It was about the cheapest in town, at 200 rupees per night. Their small home was situated in a ravine; this was where the run-off for the lake above was situated. Every morning, a cold mist would rise, covering their house and as they had no heating, it seemed to envelop

Why?

the whole property including me. Over the next few days, the damp of Kodai seemed to be seeping into my bones and with the dehydration I felt very cold. Darshan also seemed to reflect how I was feeling; somehow I had to get away from this.

Word had spread that Kodaikanal was an excellent place to get near Swami and at the same time have a holiday. So this year, VIPs appeared en masse, taking almost all the areas closest to where Baba would walk by during Darshan.

Then there was the large queue for sick people, who were always interesting to watch — as several would suddenly find the strength and good health to race each other up the steep 100 meter road, so that they could get a good place to sit while they waited on Baba to walk around. It was almost like watching a daily miracle, which only lasted until the following Darshan. So with all these extra people, it meant that getting anywhere near Baba this year was almost impossible.

As the days passed, the need to get away became stronger. I wanted to leave, but at the same time I was afraid that I would miss something. I got talking to an Australian, named John, who told me that I was definitely suffering from dehydration and that although I was drinking lots of tea and cola, they would not help to rehydrate the body. I didn't think there was such a thing as the wrong type fluid.

"The best thing that you can do mate, is get away from here for a few days."

He would be travelling to another ashram in a couple of days, which was off the mountain, and he told me that I would be welcome to travel with him. I half-heartedly said I would be interested in going. Over the next few days, I bumped into John several times and he would ask me, "Do you still want to go?"

I felt that my loyalty to Sai Baba was at stake, but then I also had a need to get away as well. I had been there for 14 days and a chill had settled into my bones; I finally decided that I couldn't stay anymore, not just for my physical health, but for my mental health as well.

The trip off the mountain is interesting in that the road is very windy and the bus drivers always seemed to be in a hurry, overtaking the taxis I had been in. I had had some heart-stopping moments, even though the taxi drivers took their time, so I had enjoyed the beautiful views and the shear drops that we often came very close too. This would be my first trip off the mountain using a bus. As I entered, the driver looked at me with his blood shot eyes and I could see he was knackered, which was not a good sign. He must have been on a timetable, as he seemed to attack the steering wheel every time there was a corner. It wasn't long before I heard several people throwing up. I tried looking at my feet, but the rocking from side to side was making me come close to losing my breakfast. Dizzy, I started to look at the furthest point on the horizon, not down – where I had seen the bus came dangerously close to the edge of a very scenic but sharp long drop.

I was sitting right at the front of the bus; unfortunately those at the back seemed to be having a harder time, as the rear bounced over every hole in the road and swung around sharp corners.

Why?

Several hours and another bus and rickshaw later, we arrived at a little orphanage/ashram. It was quite large and well-kept, with lots of plants and greenery and perhaps two dozen buildings, all with thatched roofs. The charge for staying was 10 Rupees per night (about twenty pence) and that included three meals, although I had to do two hours work in the morning and again in the late afternoon – nothing harder than watering and pruning the ashram plants.

It turned out that there was nowhere to get tea and I was avoiding sugary drinks, so I soon started to feel much better. And the deep chill I felt, quickly disappeared in the summer heat of the Indian plains.

The Swami that ran the ashram was a short and rather portly man who often walked around the ashram. The strange thing is, that when he came near me I tried to ignore him. I couldn't figure out why I did that! This was the opposite reaction to Sai Baba, which I found strange.

There were bhajans (devotional singing) several times a day. On one of these occasions, when I was sitting in a prayer hall, I had a very unusual experience.

It was as if ice-cold water had been poured into the top of my head, cooling both mind and body. I found it to be a rather refreshing experience, leaving me quite mentally peaceful for some time. Unfortunately, it only happened the once; in the heat of India, it would have been an experience that I would have enjoyed every day.

After a week, I started to make plans to return to Sai Baba. I would not go back to Kodaikanal; instead I would go directly to Whitefield and wait for Baba to come off the mountain. On my 9th day, I took a train to Whitefield.

When I got there, I found that Baba would be arriving in several hours, so my timing couldn't have been better; just managing to beat the mad crowd that would arrive shortly after Baba, all be looking for accommodation.

It was now the month of May, and I was feeling much better, as I was drinking more water and less tea. The feeling of dullness and lethargy had gone, also, I was happier and more at ease being around Baba. He had cancelled Summer Showers (the teaching course held the previous year), which pleased me immensely, and he did not go to Puttaparthi in June because of construction work going on in the Darshan hall there.

Whitefield, or more specifically, Kadugodi, where Swami's Brindavan Ashram is located, is much cooler than Puttaparthi and Bangalore is only 40 minutes away. So getting away to the city for the day is not difficult.

July was different; Gurupurnima (the day of honouring the Guru) would be on July 22nd. Gurupurnima is the opposite of Shivaratri, in that the moon is at its strongest and fullest. This day, in particular, should be spent using the strength of your mind to think of God, thus helping to tame it and keep it under control through the rest of the year.

This particular year was interesting for me, as the 22nd of July is the day that, as someone born a Leo, the sun, as the ruling planet, would enter that sign on the same day as Gurupurnima. As the celebration approached, I was told that pieces of a comet would be hit-

Why?

ting Jupiter and the last and biggest piece would hit on July 22nd.

As Jupiter is also the planet of the Guru (teacher), I felt that it would be in some way special.

The week leading up to Gurupurnima was a bit mad, as Baba had invited Bal Vikas teachers (they teach children in Sai Baba Centres, about all the different religions) from around India to the ashram for a conference. So each day, several hundred of these teachers would be given all the seating in the ashram hall and each night Baba would give a discourse. On the day of Gurupurnima, the ashram was packed; thousands had turned up by the busload. Between the morning and evening Darshans, I had been sitting cross-legged for more than seven, very squashed and painful hours. When the day was over, I decided not come back to the ashram for another Gurupurnima.

The following morning, I awoke to an amazing experience. It was as though the centre of my chest was on fire; the warmth spreading across my chest. The feeling was constant and at the same time it was as if the warmth was pulsing from my chest into my mind.

The only way I can describe it would be to say it was like a pulse of white light.

The experience was at its strongest directly after Gurupurnima. Then slowly over the next ten days, the feeling decreased in intensity until I left the ashram on the second of August.

For the entire time it was going on, I had a smile permanently stuck to my face. This was an internal joy that was complete within itself, it needed nothing. The mind merely became a witness to the experience. Each day after Gurupurnima, the intensity gradually decreased until eventually it stopped. When it was gone I felt ok. I did not miss it or long for it to happen again; I just got on with life as if nothing had happened.

On returning to the UK, it took over a month to get a job. I ended up working on the QE2 as she sailed from Southampton to New York. I was fortunate to be able to get off in New York a few times to do a bit of shopping, then after a few weeks, she sailed down to the Caribbean.

There, I managed to fulfill an old desire — to swim in a coral reef. The company gave everyone a few hours off — just enough time for some to get a drink and for me to swim in the reef.

The company had to give us some time off, as we had been working seven days a week, 10-12 hours a day, and the morale had become very low.

As we moved closer to Christmas, I started to suffer from exhaustion. Often the food on these ships for crew and contractors was not very good, and for vegetarians it was usually worse.

After two months, the long hours with few breaks were starting to take their toll on me. I finally knew it was time to leave when my head started to fall forward as I was walking along during the day. When it had happened on the fourth occasion, I thought it better to leave the job early before I had an accident; I told the foreman that I was too exhausted to carry on. The ship had sailed back across the Atlantic and was in dry dock in Hamburg, Germany, so it was quite simple for them

Why?

to arrange flights back to the UK, where I started to make yet more plans to return to India, this time for five months.

I phoned around trying to get a flight a few days before Christmas '94 so that I could join in with the celebrations, but all the flights were full on the days heading up to Christmas. I began to think that maybe I was not meant to go and started to feel very happy at that thought.

Then my insecurities kicked in, maybe Baba did not want me to go to India and maybe he was rejecting me! All of a sudden everything changed. I had to get a flight no matter the cost or when it arrived.

The only flight I could get was leaving on Christmas Eve, which meant that I would arrive in Puttaparthi on Christmas afternoon. I accepted it, strangely relieved just to be able to go.

I knew that what I had just thought and felt was odd. One minute relieved not to be going, then when I thought I was being rejected, I became glad that I could get any flight at all. I just filed the feelings away and tried to forget it, but it wouldn't go away.

When I arrived on Christmas afternoon, I had missed all of the celebrations, but the only thing I didn't miss was the large crowds, which made getting anywhere near Swami almost impossible.

A few weeks into January, most of the crowd had gone, making it easier for Baba to ignore me on a far more personal level.

By mid-January I joined an Australian group. Most of them were about my age and had a more laid back approach than most of the British groups I had observed, so I was happy to join.

I had to speak with all the group members who all agree that I could join them. Then I was told that the group had had an interview two weeks before and Swami had said to them,

"I will see you in one month".

So I started to get my hopes up that maybe this time I would get an interview.

Two weeks later, our group got a front row in the Darshan area. We all thought that maybe this would be it. As Baba came round, he stopped in front of one of the lads in the group and said,

"I've seen".

Then he walked off. Even I could not help laughing at that. Well all he had said to them was,

"I will SEE YOU in one month".

Not, "I will give you an interview".

To keep busy, I started doing some voluntary work in the museum. Although I was still in the group, I was too busy to go to the meetings, which everyone accepted. About a week after starting there I was told that the group had fallen apart because some people had left. I thought, "Ah well, that's ok". A few days later however, I was told from an original member of the group that it had re-formed with some new people.

He also told me that if I wanted to join, I would have to go to the next group meeting, which would be at 10 o'clock the next morning, to make sure it was all right with the rest of the Australians. I was happy to wait one more day.

Why?

The next morning, I was sitting in the back of the Darshan area, when I noticed that the people being called for an interview where wearing Australian scarves. I was so far back that I couldn't recognise the first few people, then I realised it was the people I was supposed to be talking to in a few hours and I hadn't even thought to bring my scarf with me to Darshan. Again, I got to watch friends go for an interview, I just could not believe what had happened. Why! There seemed to be no answer.

A few days later, some friends and I went down to see Sai Gita (Baba's pet elephant), to give her some food. I had heard that she enjoyed watermelon, so I got her a large one.

As we walked along the road to her enclosure, I was wondering how I was going to get it open, when something slammed into me from behind, spinning me around. In that instant, I heard two loud cracks in my neck, as the body went left but my head didn't.

There had been five of us going down to feed Sai Gita; two were a few metres behind me. They came rushing forward, asking me if I was ok.

I was a stunned, not sure what had just happened. Everything seemed unreal and why where they asking me if I was ok! I couldn't understand why they were concerned. Eventually, they explained to me what they had seen. A jeep that was passing had swerved from the other side of the road to deliberately hit me. There was one man hanging from the side of it and as he neared, he leant out, clipping me down the right side of my back. It was going about 20 to 30 miles per hour when it hit me.

After finding that I did not seem to have broken anything, we continued on towards Sai Gita. My problem of how to open the watermelon was solved though, for when it had fallen to the ground, it had broken into several pieces.

I believe it was very lucky that I had the watermelon in my right hand, because the weight of it was forcing my shoulder blade flat against my rib cage, so I was hit on an area that was flat and the muscles were tight from the weight of the melon.

It wasn't until later that day I started to suffer from a pain in my neck and I started to become angry, and with the anger came his friend depression.

The following day in Darshan, I got a front row by the gates. Sometimes Baba came that way, but most days he didn't. That particular day he came and stood within four to five feet of me.

I was so angry with him because I had come to India to see him and so he was somehow responsible for allowing the incident to happen. I was so angry that I came very close to actually growling at him. Someone offered him a tray of sweets; he took a handful and threw them into the crowd, all the time looking at me.

Some of the sweets fell around his feet easily within my reach. I looked at them thinking, "You can't bribe me with these bloody things". Strangely, I actually felt that he was offering me sweets to lessen my anger.

The incident had not really damaged the body, but it had certainly shaken up deep hidden emotions. Over

Why?

the next few days, I felt frustrated, angry and very tired of everything, feeling very much a victim of life. On waking on the third day, my body and mind still felt heavy and depressed; it was an effort just to get my feet off the bed just so I could sit on the edge of it. Leaning forward, I put my head in my hands and through my fingers I could see a part of a book that I had left under the bed. I reached down to get the book, thinking, "Baba, why has this happened?" I allowed pages to flick through my fingers, stopping it at a random place. The page heading was about Karma (action and reaction to one's deeds). Half-heartedly, I started reading and had got about halfway down the page, when my head spun with what I was reading.

"Your Karma is like a seed, some of it good and some bad, because of your good Karma the seeds of your bad deeds get **buried deep within the earth** so that they can't grow."

I was stunned; almost seven years previously I had a very vivid dream in which I was burning a huge python.

As I stepped back from it, the python sprouted two arms and two legs, then its eyes opened and it turned its head to me and said,

"This is the first part of your Karma. You owe me two more".

When it had finished speaking, the dream froze and I heard a woman's voice behind me saying,

"Don't worry, the other two parts of the **Karma are buried deep within the earth**".

At the time of the dream, I had just met Charles and I had no idea what Karma meant or the burying deep within the earth, but after all these years it would seem that something else was now finished from my past and the worst of what could have happened in that moment would not grow any further. When I considered what had happened when I was hit from behind, I did think of myself as being very lucky. Given the speed the driver was doing when he hit me, spinning the body round, it should have snapped my neck, however, the effect of the accident was more emotional than physical.

It took almost a month to get over the emotions that it stirred up from within and by Shivaratri; I was not feeling too bad. I was looking forward to it after last year's experience.

On the morning of the festival, I had got a front row seat. I became so relaxed as I waited for Baba that I started to feel and hear the beat of my heart as it vibrated throughout my whole body.

As this was happening, Baba came out. I was watching him and at the same time relaxing into the feeling of the beat of the heart, when for a moment it stopped. The only thing that moved were my eyes as they followed Baba, then it started again with the same feeling throughout my body for a while longer.

Maybe it was my imagination, maybe it was not, but it definitely was a strange, enjoyable and very relaxing Shivaratri.

After Shivaratri, Swami would usually go to Whitefield, as Puttaparthi starts to get very hot, but this year was the run up to Baba's 70th birthday, so he stayed on

Why?

for another month to make arrangements for the celebration, eventually leaving in the first week of April.

I don't think I've ever been so hot.

By midday, I had to walk from one shaded area to another. To sleep in the evening, I had to soak a sheet and sleep right under the room fan, so that I could get cool enough to drop off.

There was a lot of gossip about when Baba would be going to Whitefield. It seemed everyone had a great source, usually from someone on the veranda. But none of this gossip turned out to be true. When Baba did leave for Whitefield, everyone was about gossiped-out, or just plain embarrassed that they had all got it so wrong. The day before Baba did leave, the person that washed my clothes told me,

"Baba's leaving tomorrow".

I smiled, but did not believe him. However, it turned out that the only good source of information around the ashram was the Dhobi man (clothes washer).

By the time I arrived at Whitefield I was not feeling very well emotionally. Over the years I had been coming, I had watched literally hundreds of people being called by Baba for interviews and there were some groups that seemed to have their own walkway straight in.

Watching all this and being physically ignored for so long had been difficult for me.

And here he was doing it again with two Italians who were about the same age as me. I watched as every day they where called in for an interview. In Darshan, Baba was constantly turning his back on me as he came close and then to top it off, I had a dream of him in which he was calling people in front of me then behind me, not even glancing in my direction. So even in my dreams I was being ignoring, all of which only added to some very intense feelings, which I was trying my best to hide/ignore.

Again, this year at Brindavan, everyone was told to move out of the ashram, as there was going to be another Summer Showers Course. Again Baba would be giving discourses to his students, their parents and some lucky devotees who managed to get passes; and I wasn't to be one of them!

Many people had to leave the ashram to make room for the students. Although at the time I was already living outside, it still managed to stir up feelings of rejection. The Darshan was again very short, mostly consisting of Swami getting out of his car, waving to the crowd, then getting back in and driving off to give his students a discourse.

Calling the event 'Summer Showers' is very apt, as it is usually raining a lot around that time of the year.

Baba eventually left for Puttaparthi in June and I very reluctantly followed, hoping that I would change or something would change with my relationship with Baba. Unfortunately it remained the same and when my time came to leave, I was relieved and very happy that this trip was over. After six months of too much sun, I was looking forward to a typical British summer (cool, with rain). And I hoped I would not need to return to India.

Why?

It was now late June and Britain was unfortunately having a heat wave, I thought that I would have some time off before starting a new job. My brother Liam had just been offered some work fitting out a pub, so the day before he was due to start; we went along to see what stage the refit was at.

As I was with him, I decided just to have a look. I got talking to the site foreman and he asked me what I did. I told him, "I am a carpenter" and he replied that the company needed more carpenters for another job in the New Forest. Before I knew what was happening, I was being talked into a job that I didn't want to do.

I tried to make some excuses; the first was that I had no transport. My brother immediately said, "That's OK, this job's only five minutes away from the house, I can take my bike and you can have the car".

No matter what excuse I made, the pair of them countered it, so I found myself reluctantly being talked into starting work the next day, which was just as well as I had a lot less money in the bank than I thought. By the time the first pay cheque went in, I had just gone overdrawn.

It was also nice to go into a pub and get some money out instead of leaving it behind the bar.

Liam and I eventually ended up working together for the company, doing several pub refits until the end of the year. Fortunately, whatever it was that was happening at the ashram was definitely making me happier and easer to be around in normal life.

As each new job came around, I noticed that I was much more comfortable with other people and more at ease with life. The little things that upset me just did not matter anymore. It seemed that each time I left the ashram, my ability to deal with life leaped forward after having been so emotionally stretched.

The last job I did with Liam that year was due to stop for Christmas. I had been planning on going back to India in March or April for six months, but at Christmas the weather took a turn for the worse, hitting -22° in Glasgow and according to the weather forecasts, it was coming south.

So I thought, "I can stay here on a job with no roof and freeze, then go to India after winter for six months, returning in time for next winter, or, I can go now for four months and return to the UK for the beginning of summer".

When I thought of it like that, there was no real choice, so by 8th January, I was back in the ashram in the hot weather and I would be returning to the UK in early May.

As soon as I returned, I started to have difficulty being at the ashram; all I wanted to do was leave, but to where? There was nothing in India that I had the slightest interest in, nowhere I wanted to go, but the place I did not want to be was Puttaparthi. I felt trapped.

Then to top it off, the two Italians that were there on my last trip turned up. I was still trying to deal with seeing more of Baba's back and the feelings that it caused. I knew the moment I saw them that they would be having lots of interviews and my heart sank. Sure enough,

Why?

the following morning Baba stopped in front of them, then they stood up and headed for the interview room.

For me this was just too much. The emotions it brought up were strong enough for me to finally decide to leave. Up until this point, I had always felt trapped, afraid to leave, but this had pushed me beyond that point. I went back to my room to pack my bag and got the next bus out of Puttaparthi for Bangalore.

I decided that I would go to Kerala in the south of India. On my arrival in Bangalore, I purchased a train ticket for the following night and then went shopping on Brigade Road. There, I met a German woman. We started to talk and got on very well. We hung out for the rest of the day and when she asked me if I would like to meet her for breakfast the next day, I thought, "Well it's not that often that an attractive woman asks me for breakfast", so I accepted.

I cancelled my ticket to Kerala. We met the next day and again, the conversation got round to relationships, she asked if I was single, which I was and I told her so. Then I asked,

"What about you?"

" Yes I'm single and a lesbian."

I was so surprised, I came out with an all-time-classic stupid reply,

"Are you sure?"

"Of course."

Before she had answered, I was thinking I should crawl under a rock or put both hands on my head and say,

"O God, I didn't just say that".

Instead I kept a small smile on my face in the vane hope that she thought I was only joking and hoped she was; she wasn't though.

To say I was a little disappointed would be an understatement. We spent the rest of the day together and in some ways we became more open and friendlier. The next day she went north and I went back to the ashram, smiling most of the way. Meeting her was just what I needed; a bit of a tonic. I am sure that when God was giving out brains, he forgot some of mine. When I was asked by friends why I had returned, I told them a very funny story.

The two Italians had several more interviews, which after Bangalore did not upset me at all, and the intensity of feeling ignored by Baba was more bearable.

A few weeks later, Shivaratri started. After the last two unusual ones, I had been looking forward to this celebration again. I was expecting something to happen, but this time I felt nothing. I had been sitting painfully for about four and a half hours. Two and a half hours waiting for Baba, then two hours listening to Swami's students sing — and I must admit over the past few years they had been getting better. When they had sung in previous years, it was almost painful for me to listen.

When the morning Darshan had finished, I needed to go straight to the toilet. On leaving the toilet I failed to notice a concrete overhang, as I was looking down and was wearing a hat. So I walked straight into it, hitting myself on the very top of my head.

I did not damage the concrete, but I was seeing stars. Several people, on hearing the noise my head made

Why?

asked if I was all right? I was too embarrassed and said that I was fine, with a very weak smile.

I went back to my room to lie down. It was not until sometime afterwards that I understood I was in fact going in and out of consciousness, which went on for the rest of the day. For the next week I had a mild headache and occasionally I would get a stabbing pain in the top of my head, almost as if someone had thrust a knife into it. I was told a few times to go and see a doctor, which would have been the smart thing to do, but I've not always been the smartest person around.

Again after Shivaratri, Swami went to Whitefield and for the first time, I started to do some regular volunteer work in the kitchen. Veronica, the woman who ran it, gave me a pass that allowed me to sit in the reserved block with the VIPs.

This was great, as it meant not having to sit in the token lines, but I could not sit front row; but that was fine. Just to have the consistency of knowing where I would sit was good for calming the mind. The whole month that I was there, it didn't matter which part of the block I sat, as Swami would pass at the furthest point to where I was, but because there was a consistency it did not seem to matter quite as much. Normally, I would have to sit in the token lines, which meant there was never any permanent place where I would be, this always seemed to keep the mind off balance.

At the end of the month, Baba went to Kodaikanal. I went up a day early by train to get away from the mad rush, so when everyone arrived I was already settled in.

Cooling Fire

Again that year, there were a lot of VIPs, so the closest I could hope to get near Baba was about five or six rows from the front. Therefore, most days I slipped in at the back just before Baba came out.

Each evening he was giving a discourse. Even though I considered Baba to be a divine incarnation, I found the discourse very boring, as the speaker system was not very good, making it almost impossible to follow the translator. I know that Baba had said to people who don't speak English that it's not so much the discourse that's important, it's being in his presence for longer that will change you.

So after a month of seemingly being more bored than changed, I heard a rumor that Baba was going back to Whitefield. Without hesitation, I made arrangements to return to Baba's Whitefield ashram in Bangalore. It turned out to be wrong, as almost all rumours around Baba usually are.

I was in Whitefield for several days before Swami returned. I filled in the time by helping to clean the kitchen with some people who had heard the same rumours. When Swami did arrive, I left the day after for the UK, glad to be leaving again.

Why?

Chapter Nine

Why, Why, Why

Through the remainder of '96, I worked on several different carpentry jobs, often having to travel around the UK. By October, I decided to go to Scotland to see some of my family. Once there, I got in contact with some people I had met at the ashram and was told that I might be able to get a five-year visa for India in Glasgow; something that was impossible to get at the High Commission in London. I decided to try for one.

At that particular time I had no desire to go anywhere near Baba. I just wanted the visa for some time in the future; hopefully in the distant future. Life was good and my mind seemed more at peace than it ever had been. I did not get a five-year visa, but was given one for a year. I was only given that after I had talked to the man in charge of the High Commission in some depth about why I had been going to India so much and about my experiences around Sai Baba. Happily, my explanation impressed him enough for him to grant me a one-year visa instead of the six-month that he explained I was allowed.

The moment the visa was in my passport, I started to get itchy feet. I had been trying to stay as far away from

India as possible. Life was going well and I could not remember the last time I had a more money in my bank account, so going back to India was at the bottom of my 'to do' list; but a part of me wanted to return. I tried my hardest not think about it, but the pull to go back was becoming stronger by the day. It wasn't just a thought, it was a feeling like being torn inside, a compulsion I had to go back. The feelings only eased when I booked the ticket, so just after a week of getting my visa, I was back in India again, with a one-year visa and enough money for at least eight months or more. I was amazed at my own stupidity for what I had done!

It was just after the middle of October when I arrived. It did not take me very long to settle in, but after all the previous times I had stayed in India, this time it was much tougher. The accumulated times of feeling that for some reason Baba was rejecting me were taking their toll.

When I arrived, there was a large group that were doing a play. Each day they would rehearse in the Poornachandra Hall. Often Baba would be late into the Darshan area, as he would be at their rehearsals, meaning the time we sat waiting was much longer.

Also, each day Baba gave them an interview, sometimes two. If he did not give the second interview, he would always stop and talk to them.

In many ways I thought that I was totally detached from what I was seeing each day. I remember seeing them in the canteen and noticing that all of them had been given some piece of jewellery from Baba. I looked at one man's ring, which had rubies set in the shape of

Why?

an 'Om' surrounded by diamonds. I thought I felt nothing; almost empty, but a long time afterwards I realised I had somehow created a barrier between what the eye saw and the mind would accept. Thereby, I was able to deny any feelings I had about the attention they were getting.

This went on for about two weeks. Twice each day, I had been sitting waiting cross-legged for 2-3 hours (that's normal) for Baba to come out and my body was feeling every minute of it.

Then one afternoon before Baba even came out to give Darshan, he had the security call the group in for an interview. So everyone would have to wait at least another 30 minutes before Baba had finished with them. Eventually he came out at 4:30, rather than normal — which was between 3:45 and 3:55 p.m.

As he came past me, I could see what I thought was a look of anger on his face, but straight away I knew that what I was seeing was a reflection of me. I thought, "No. I am not angry!"

Yet I knew it had to be me, but how? I wanted to deny it, but I knew it had to be a part of me. On leaving Darshan I kept thinking, "Why? Why? Why do you give to others so much and to me you just give an angry look? Why? Why?"

As I was returning to my room, I tried to put a meaning to what was going on. Why did he give so much attention to others but to me he would turn his back and give a look of anger? Why? Why?

When I got to my room I picked up a picture of Baba and as I looked at it I kept thinking, "Why? Why? Why?"

Then I had a feeling of absolute certainty that I was not going to be told. My mind felt so clear, I knew then that I would be wasting my time staying. I had come to a point where I had hit a wall; I could go no further with Sai Baba. I could feel the wall in my mind that stopped me from growing any more. There and then I decided I should leave.

I took my flight ticket to an agent outside the ashram and asked them to change my dates. In a few weeks it would be Baba's birthday, so I thought out of respect for Baba and for all that he had done for me, I would stay until after his birthday on November 23rd.

As I was returning to the ashram, I met a friend and I told him,

"I've had enough, I am off to the UK".

His reply was,

"Why? Why? Why?" I couldn't help but be amazed that it was the same question I had just been asking, but this time I got the answer. The feelings of rejection that I had been hiding all my life came flooding back. It took everything I had, just to stop from bursting into tears. A lifetime of holding onto a wall that hid so much pain behind it was about to be exposed. The wall I had felt earlier in my room was about to be ripped away.

Everything that Baba had been doing over the years was similar to what had happened to me in my childhood. Baba had given the others attention; he had presented them with gifts; he had taken them away and not

Why?

me. He had turned his back on me when I thought I needed him most. I had bottled up all the feelings and hid them so well that even I did not know what I had been hiding all my life.

My friend noticed my reaction and said,

"Let's go for a cup of tea".

I could only nod my head, so we went to a cafe nearby. I sat for only a few minutes. Each time I tried to speak, I almost started to cry, so I decided to go to my room in the ashram.

On the way there, I saw the German man, Gert, who I had been sharing the room with. He was standing at a corner, looking towards the room, then towards the shops trying to make a decision. He kept looking in both directions several times before walking off to the shops. I was relieved. I knew I needed to be alone.

Once in my room, the emotions that I had been hiding for so many years quite literally exploded from the body. All the pain I had ever suppressed was trying to leave the body at the same time.

I sat on the edge of my bed hugging myself as every muscle locked, tears running freely down my face, my mouth wide open silently screaming as the pain washed out. But there was not enough air in my lungs to finish the never-ending scream. At times, I had to gasp for breath, as the body only wanted to push out, not draw in something new in. I could only manage small, sharp gulps of air as the silent scream just went on and on and on. The intensity of the emotions was stopping any real sound from coming out of my throat.

Why, Why, Why

Intermittently, the torture seemed to stop and I would try to get up, only for it to start all over again, the intensity the same as the moment it had started.

I suppose this went on for less than an hour, but by the time it had finished, my whole body felt like a raw nerve. I had just been emptied of a huge burden, but now I was left empty; devoid of any feelings, a dull, almost heavy sensation that left me with little interest in anything.

For the first time, I could now see how far Baba would take a person in order to release the pain that had been hidden within. He had pushed me to a place where I had broken.

Over the next few days I told anyone that would listen that Baba had mirrored my relationship with my father ignoring me to a point that all the emotions had exploded from the body. Unfortunately, I said it in such a miserable, depressed way that after just a few days, some people started to avoid me.

I did not realise it at the time, but I was laying the blame for what had happened firmly on my father and Baba. But within a week, I had a dream in which I walked up to an opening and as I looked in, there were about 30 large mirrors that formed a complete circle; apart from the place that I was standing.

I was confused because none of the mirrors reflected my image. Instead, in each mirror there was an image of Baba, then I heard his voice to my left, I turned in surprise, realising that in one of the openings was baba – not a reflection. I suddenly realised that there was some-

Why?

thing wrong with everything I was seeing, the refections weren't reflections after all.

I awoke more troubled and confused than I already was, knowing that I was mistaken when I had been telling people that Baba was reflecting my relationship with my father.

I knew that when I looked in a mirror, the only reflection I should have seen was me. With no one to blame for what had happened, I had to just shut up and get on with how I felt.

A few days later, I had another dream, which helped me to understand some of what was going on. I was standing inside a house looking out of the window. Directly in front of the house was a large mountain, which blocked my view so much that I could see nothing else.

I watched as a torrent of water started to rush past the house, hitting the base of the mountain. The force of the water was so great, that as it hit the base it went vertical for several hundred feet. I turned to someone behind me, saying that the force of the water would destroy the mountain. As I turned back, the water had started to bore a hole into the side of the mountain. I knew the pressure must have been immense. Then the whole mountain exploded, with debris falling all around.

Then it was all gone. I could see as far as the horizon with gently rolling hills and everything had a crystal clarity about it.

On waking, I knew that the mountain represented an emotional block that was obscuring how I perceived the world and the water represented the strength of emotion that would need to build up within to create enough pressure to destroy and remove the mountain that was obscuring how I saw the world. Although the pain had been released, I was still living through the shock of the experience.

I became withdrawn for several months, as I seemed to pull within myself to contain the hurt I had just felt.

I slowly came to realise that in some way I was trying to blame my father, using him as an emotional crutch — someone to blame other than myself for the pain I was now feeling. The first dream stopped that way of thinking in its tracks and I believe that in some way, it helped along the healing of the emptiness I was feeling.

It had taken Baba four years of constantly chipping away and applying pressure to the pain for it to be released. Now, even more, all I wanted was to get as far away from this place as possible. Every other day, I would go to the agent's office, hoping that he would have a flight date for me to leave India. It took two weeks to finally get a confirmation for just after Baba's birthday. When I was handed my ticket I was glad to be going, but the moment I stepped out of the office I knew, if I left I would be running away from how I was feeling. I could not do that, no matter how much I disliked the thought of staying. I could not run away, I had to stay. I took a deep breath, turned around and stepped back into the office, my mind raced, "I won't stay for eight months, I'll stay for five". So I said to the man I had been harassing for the past two weeks,

"Can you change the dates on my ticket again?"

Why?

To give him credit, he only paused for a moment before saying,

"Yes, when do you want to leave?"

"March."

"Any particular date?"

"No, just any time in March."

Although I had decided to stay, I was having a very hard time. My sense of discipline had gone. In some ways, I became very hard on myself and often quite cynical about other people's nice experiences. I often said to people, "I don't care", but really I did, it was the only way I had of dealing with how I felt. It didn't help that many people would say,

"Ah, Baba will do something to help you".

Well, as far as I was concerned, he had, and how I was feeling was the consequence of that.

I went to Darshan every day, going in at the last moment. Once or twice a week I tried to make an effort to get out of the mental rut I was in by going to the token lines for Darshan; maybe Baba would do something, but I would always ended up at the back. Then I would give up trying for a while and slip back into a state of lethargy.

At the beginning of December, preparations for Christmas and the children's play started. After much reluctance, I was persuaded to join in. I ended up taking props on and off stage.

On one occasion, Swami came out to see how things were getting on, he stopped and spoke to several people; and then as he was about to leave, he stopped in front of the small group helping with the props.

He was only about four feet from me when he asked the person two places to my left,

"Where are you from?"

"Australia, Swami."

"Very happy", said Baba.

Then, to the person standing at my right,

"Where are you from?"

"Canada, Swami."

Again Baba said,

"Very happy."

Then, to the person standing to the left,

"Where are you from?"

"Australia, Swami."

"Very happy."

I thought at that moment that he was about to speak to me for the first time, but as he said his last, "Very happy", he turned and walked away.

At that moment I got a rush of energy to my head, this filled my mind and body with warmth and peace, but within 20 minutes I had pushed the experience aside and was thinking more about why he had spoken to the others and not to me. I was aware that maybe I had been given more in that moment of being ignored than maybe all those he had spoken to, but I wasn't at that time prepared to admit that to anyone. All I could think of was that he was still going out of his way to ignore me.

The play itself was a good distraction for me. Unfortunately, the rehearsals and play finished on the 24th of December. So by the end of the year, with no focus of

Why?

discipline to help fill my time, I again quickly lost all enthusiasm for just about everything.

By mid February, I knew that I had to get out of the mental and emotional rut I was in, so I decided no matter what, I would start going to the token lines.

Sure enough the first day I got a high token number just like all the other times that I had tried, but this time I told myself, it's okay, it doesn't matter whether I am in front or in the back, just as long as I manage not to fall back into the lethargy and depression that had plagued me since the beginning of November.

Although I had managed to stay positive through Darshan, I was still afraid of falling back into where I had been mentally, but today was the right day to be positive.

As I was leaving the Darshan hall, I heard someone call my name. I turned and there were a few people with tartan scarves.

"Hi Arthur", I said.

"Joe, good, I have brought a scarf for you."

"How did you know I was even here?"

"You're always here. Meet me later and I'll give you a group scarf."

Arthur was from Scotland and we had met a few times over the years.

The group was just what I needed and they would be in the ashram for ten days. In the ten days that they were there, the group was fortunate to get first and second rows every day, on one occasion Swami stopped in front of Arthur, the man who had arranged the group, and asked him,

"Where are you from?"

I was sitting about ten people away and could hear him clearly, Arthur had to ask him to repeat himself and after Arthur had answered, Baba produced some Vibhuti for him then walked off.

When I met him the next day, he told me that he had woken in the middle of the night desperate to go to the toilet and when he woke this morning the swollen ankles he had had for several years had returned to normal and a skin disorder he had also had for years had drastically improved overnight.

Some days after that, the group were sitting in the second row, Swami stopped almost in front of me and as he looked over my head, he said quite loudly,

"Tomorrow".

For a moment, I thought he was talking to me, then I thought, "I bet he's talking to the remainder of the group that had been doing the play back in November". So I turned round just to check and sure enough, the last two men from the group where waving at Baba. Still, I felt that in some way it was also meant for me.

As I was walking out of the Darshan area, an Indian that was in my group said to me,

"Baba said to you 'tomorrow', so we will get an interview".

"No, he was talking to someone behind me."

But he didn't seem convinced and neither was I. Because of all the let down that I had felt over the years, I was not about to get excited over something that might not even happen.

Why?

The following morning, the group got yet another front row. I sat wondering if something was about to happen, then I was momentarily disturbed as the second row started to fill, someone had just put their knee into my back, not an unusual thing to happen. I glanced around to see the two men that Baba had spoken to the day before, each one with a knee at the centre of my back. It was then that I knew something was going to happen.

As Swami came around he stopped in front of me and started to talk to them, at the same time he was leaning over me and standing on my leg. I could feel energy-like waves washing up through the body into my mind, causing a state of euphoria. I felt as if there was so much energy washing into me that I was going to burst at any moment.

I have no idea how long he stood there or what he was talking about. As Baba walked away, the experience stopped and I immediately felt normal. I wanted it to continue, but with Baba I guess I would only get what I needed. It was enough to change me. The discipline of the Scottish group had helped me immensely, as well as whatever had happened when Baba had stood on my leg. The lethargy and dullness had receded and I was left with a better perspective on being around Baba. My mind had been lifted out of the depression it had been wallowing in for the past several months.

I stayed on for another month after the Scottish group left. In that time, I only managed one more front row and the two Italians turned up and got some more interviews, but I didn't really care at the time.

Why, Why, Why

When I returned to the UK, I got into a relationship. In many ways we were very compatible, having similar interests and both being vegetarians, but within a few weeks I had to go on a job in Holland. I phoned most days and I was only there for a month.

Before I had met her, I had already made some plans to return to India in July, the reason being that the bhajan group that I went to in Southampton was going and also that the trip would be during my birthday. So I returned to India.

I offered to pay for her flight, but she was at that time buying a flat and could not take the time off work. So I went alone. My trip this time was for only three weeks and that was all I wanted it to be.

When I returned to India, I was very wary of getting too involved or even getting anywhere near to Baba, just in case there was still some more pain that had to be removed. So almost the whole time I was there I was trying to stay as far away from Baba as possible, trying not to be there, hoping that the end would come soon.

Three weeks was the shortest stay that I'd had at the ashram and compared to the other stays, it was almost like having a holiday. The end of the stay did not come quickly enough and I was very happy to leave.

I arrived back in the UK on the 8th of August, and the moment I left the aeroplane an overwhelming feeling hit me.

"I have to go back, I have to complete something."

I tried to ignore it, but the more I did, the more everything felt wrong.

Why?

As the days went by, the feeling became too strong to ignore. I just had to go back; I had to complete something. Reluctantly I gave into it, it was only then that the levels of stress started to reduce, but my girlfriend was not so understanding. I could not describe to her the intensity of the feeling that was driving me back to India.

On August 20th, just 12 days after leaving the ashram I was back! And I felt somewhat more relaxed being there. In the middle of my stay, there would be a large festival and I would not be involved. So instead of staying around and feeling left out. I decided it would be a good time to visit a dentist in Bangalore. Besides, I thought a visit to the dentist would be much less painful than staying around Sai Baba during a festival.

I started to arrange for some accommodation, making several calls to hotels in the city.

I got an answer from one that had some rooms available at that time, so I asked to book one. I was surprised to be told abruptly,

"Phone again in the morning".

Then he hung up. Since it was a very good hotel, I tried again in the morning, then in the afternoon and then for the next couple of days. No one answered the phone.

The festival was almost upon me when I finally got through. I asked if they still had rooms,

"Yes sir", came the reply.

"Could I book two, maybe three days please."

"We don't take bookings for such short periods."
And he hung up without another word.

Why, Why, Why

It left me bemused, I could see the funny side of it and I had come to accept the often strange, at least to me, Indian-style way of communicating.

I returned to the ashram and was telling a Canadian friend, Sam, some of what had just happened, when an older English lady approached me saying,

"Ah, Joe, can you help me?"

In the past I had a habit of saying "NO" to people and then asking what they wanted. Just then I was trying to break that bad habit. So I immediately said, "Yes" without asking what she wanted of me.

"I want you to be my partner for the Paduka Ceremony."

This meant I would have to be part of the very ceremony (Puja) that I would have been happier having my teeth drilled rather than stay around for.

"Stay there and I will go and get your dhoti", (a man's wrap-around, skirt-like garment) and without another word, she sped off to her room.

At that, I turned to Sam.

"Did she say dhoti?"

But he was already laughing. This was something that in the years that I had been going to India, I had chosen not wear under any circumstances. As Sam had known my feelings about this type of clothing, it took him a while to stop laughing before he could say with a big smile,

"Yes".

This was exactly what I was going to the dentist to avoid.

Why?

It also meant I would have to be sitting in the Darshan area for a ceremony (Puja) that would last at least four or five hours.

The ashram observes most religious ceremonies of the different religions. I had never been involved with any of them so far and there had been lots of them. To me, it generally meant a larger crowed and a time to avoid.

This ceremony was a Paduka Puja, a ritual involving symbolic sandals that represent those worn by the Rama Avatar. The event took two days, the first day the couples went in to the Darshan with the Padukas. I ended up about two-thirds of the way up, on what would normally the ladies side of the Darshan area. I couldn't help but notice that from their section the women have a much better view than on the men's side.

The ritual went on for over four hours, with priests constantly chanting mantras.

At certain stages we were told to put various items on the sandals, in effect sanctifying them. Baba had come out to the crowd several times, although each time he made a smaller pass on my side, by the third time he didn't even come to my side. At that, I must have tapped in to all the ladies' feelings that he always gave the men more attention (which he did), as a strange thought popped into my head,

"Typical, he's always on the men's side".

I understood that these were definitely some stray thoughts left around from when the women were normally there.

213

During the Puja, there was a very strange, almost tingling sensation in my head, but as I was too busy trying to put the various items on the sandals, I had no time to think about it.

The second day I had to wear the dhoti. There were several thousand couples, the women looked good, all with the same saris, but most of the men looked like a bag of potatoes tied at the waist.

It's surprising how many Indian men don't know how to wear their own traditional clothing. I ended up asking for help from a white American, as all the Indians I knew didn't have a clue how to wear it.

The procession went through the ashram to the main hall where Swami came out and threw rice. As he passed me a grain of rice landed inside my ear. My partner then asked if I had got hold of any rice, which I then produced for her by tilting my head forward and to one side and plucking a single grain from the inside of my ear.

After the ceremony, my mind felt healed and the feeling of loss that I carried since the year before was just gone. I felt much more at peace and happy, somehow the energy from this strange ceremony had healed my pain and taken away the final parts of the darkness from my mind.

When I returned to the UK in October, I made a few phone calls, slowly going through the list of companies I had worked for in the past, but they all said there was nothing at the moment. There was only one company I had not phoned, mainly because I had phoned them so many times over the year and they always said, "No".

Why?

Well, I had nothing to lose but the cost of a call, fortunately they just happened to be looking for people for a job in Malta, which would start in another two weeks. As it had to do with work, my girlfriend was OK with me going off yet again.

Before I went away this time, I had begun to feel that our relationship would not work long term and it did not help that by the time I had finished the job in Malta I had decided to go to India again.

She believed I was running away to,

"That bloody holy man!"

Of course, she was right, and without hesitating, she ended the relationship.

Because of my last visit, I believed that the worst was over, so I thought that I would return for another long stay, December through to the beginning of March. I also hoped that after all that I had gone through, I might get an interview, but again that was not to happen.

Within a few days of being there, I had finally got a front row seat in Darshan, when Baba came past he did what he had been doing for the past couple of years; he kept his back to me as he walked along the other side, taking letters from people. After he was gone, I started to think that the only way I was ever going to get an interview was to stand up and walk in without him inviting me.

I then started to imagine walking up into the interview room, creating in my head a very clear image, getting to the place on the veranda where I had seen so many people sit before going in for a interview.

At the moment I reached that point, I felt a terrifying fear of being rejected. I was not just afraid of being rejected, I was terrified.

I touched a fear deep inside of me that was so real I was almost sick, every nerve in my body aflame with the fear that I might be rejected, I could even taste it in my mouth.

I tried for the next couple of days to get over the fear, sometimes trying to stand up and walk in, but each time I did that, the fear would be there and it was far stronger and more painful than my resolve to face it.

At the same time, I also tried to get over it mentally, analysing it, dissecting it, trying to put it in some sort of perspective, but still that was not enough, I could still feel it each day.

So I continued to mentally batter myself. This I had to get over, I could no longer ignore what I felt. Eventually I gave up accepting it was there, knowing that I could do nothing about it except write a letter to Baba explaining what I had seen in myself — that I was not capable of overcoming the fear myself and that I was giving it to him to deal with.

Straight away, he took the letter and the thoughts and feelings I had been having just melted away. So I got on with being in the ashram, but what I didn't know was that I was about to live through that fear.

On the morning of the 19th of December I had a very powerful dream.

I was walking along in the Darshan area when I bumped into an elderly man. We both started to fall and as we did, I began to plead in my mind,

Why?

"Baba, Please don't hurt him".

As we fell, I said it over and over again. I also tried to twist as we were falling so that he would land on top of me. As we hit the ground, he started to have a heart attack and he died. This happened while he was still on my chest. I awoke abruptly with an overwhelming sense of loss and could physically feel pain where he had landed on my chest.

I knew straight away that something very old inside of me had died — something that I no longer needed.

Knowing that didn't lessen the sense of loss that I felt, as if someone, something close to me had died.

I slept for perhaps 20 of the next 24 hours and that was after having had a full night's sleep before that.

Again, being around Baba became very difficult. The discipline that I had regained on the last trip soon deserted me, making going to Darshan very difficult. With Christmas coming up I felt no enthusiasm for taking part in the celebrations, so I ended up missing most of it.

After the New Year, the feeling of loss was still very strong until the second day of January.

As Baba came around the Darshan area, he stopped in front of a friend of mine, telling him to go for an interview. On seeing this, a feeling of emptiness seemed to open up inside of me, then I watched another person get up from the back of the Darshan area that I also knew, then another. Each time the feeling within me intensified and before I knew what was going on, I had stood up and was walking in as well.

Why, Why, Why

The whole time my mind was empty of thoughts, it was like being on autopilot. I was just doing it, but I felt strangely sensitive to everything around me.

As I neared the door to the interview room, I passed a pillar and there on my left was Baba about five feet away, looking directly at me.

By then I had joined the end of the line that was going inside for the interview. Baba turned to the person in front of me and said,

"Who is this boy?"

Out of the corner of my eye I could see the person in front of me looking over his shoulder.

Still looking at Baba I managed to say,

"UK, Swami".

He then said loudly,

"GO NOW".

As I turned to leave, Baba had already taken several steps towards me and smiling, he had raised his arm above his head. By then I was already side onto him and he lowered his arm in a sweeping motion down the length of my back, without actually touching me.

I hesitated for a moment, but that feeling of being on autopilot was still there, so I continued to walk away feeling incredibly sensitive to everything around me.

Sai Baba must have entered the interview room, as everyone started to stand. I felt it more as a wave of energy that seemed rise through my body. As I reached the side gate, others were already leaving and as I passed the threshold of the gates going to the Darshan area, I felt an incredible pain at the base of my spine. It was as if someone had hit me with a hammer.

Why?

I knew that if I stopped at this moment I would collapse with the pain. I just kept thinking, "Don't stop, don't stop! Keep moving". I headed back to my room focusing only on getting one foot in front of the other. Even when I got to the room I kept thinking, "Just do something", so I started to scrub some clothes that I had left soaking the night before. It helped to keep my mind blank. At some point, I became aware that physically and mentally I had relaxed. I left the bathroom area and sat in the middle of the room. I had calmed down enough to think about what just happened. I felt no rejection from Baba.

"Okay, he said, 'Go now'".

"OK, I'll leave."

I knew the moment I thought that, it was not what he had meant.

He meant, "Go into the interview room!"

But that wasn't right either. Then I realised that what he meant was the fear that the body had been holding onto the pain that I had offered to him earlier that month.

"Go now."

He was talking about something in that moment.

As he brushed his hand down my back, he was telling the pain to simply go away.

I had known for some time that the body somehow manages to hold on to fear and pain, locking it away in the base of the spine. The physical pain I experienced the moment I crossed the threshold of the Darshan area should have been happening from the moment I originally stood up in the Darshan area. However, I had been protected from the pain and allowed to face my worst fear without experiencing the worst of the pain that the body would throw up as a barrier.

Although I had faced a great fear within myself, my sense of inner balance was now gone, so sitting in the queues became difficult yet again. I was very much out of sorts with myself and also a little bit afraid of what Baba might do to me next. What more lay hidden within? So I reduced my stay in India by a month and God, was I glad to leave.

Chapter Ten

Running Away Again

On my return to the UK, I ended up back in my old relationship again. Even as I was getting back into it, I knew that what I was doing was wrong. I was at odds with myself as to why I was doing this. I had still not found a new balance within myself since my last trip to India and this meant that I had difficulty focusing on anything for any real length of time.

I started to work locally with my brother Liam, fitting out a luxury yacht. The quality of workmanship on this job was by far the highest that I had ever worked on, I had only been on the job for about a month, but I was already itching for something else. One Monday morning Liam had an appointment at the hospital and as he was driving me to the job, we would be going in late that day. Half-heartedly, I made some phone calls that morning to see if there was any other work around. There seemed to be nothing.

I desperately needed a change. I felt dejected and gave up. Reluctantly, I went to prepare my lunch.

As I entered the kitchen I just thought, "I'm going to India, I've got just enough money for a month, I can go". My only doubt was that maybe my visa was not valid.

Running Away Again

If it was not, then the extra expense of going to London for a visa would mean that I would have to abandon the whole idea. My passport was somewhere in my bedroom, so I went in search of it.

As I passed my sister-in-law in the living room I said,

"I've decided, if my visa is still valid, then I'm off to India again".

She smiled and said,

"Typical".

After all, it was not the first time I had just dropped everything and left for India.

When I finally found my passport, there was just over a month left to run on the visa, so I started to make phone calls again, but this time for flights. It would mean that I would be broke again when I returned, but I just had to get away. I managed to confirm a flight for Wednesday – less than 48 hours away. I did not realise it at the time, but I was trying to run away from the pain I still felt from the last trip to India.

It was now late April 1998 and Baba would be at his Brindavan Ashram, just 30 minutes outside of Bangalore City. I arrived on Thursday morning, physically and emotionally weary.

What would I learn about myself this time and would it be as painful as the last time? But being there this time was different from the other visits. There was still the usual token system for where I would be sitting in the Darshan area, but I kept getting front rows.

The other thing that helped was that almost every other day I was in Bangalore shopping or eating; any-

Why?

thing that would mean I would not have to be hanging around the ashram all day. But Baba seemed to be going out of his way to take letters from me, almost all of which were about why I kept getting back into a relationship that I knew was not working, an addiction that I could see was hurting someone else. Not surprisingly, my girlfriend said the relationship was over again.

Although I had spent most days in Bangalore, I started to believe that my relationship with Baba had turned a corner and finally the worst was over. It's difficult to explain, but many small things had happened over the month between Baba and I that allowed me to become more relaxed. I began to believe that with so much of my past pain dealt with, my future could only get better.

When I returned to the UK, I again got back into the old relationship and was amazed at my own madness. I still don't know why or how she ever put up with me. We had only been back together for a week, when I was offered a good paying job in Cornwall; it would mean travelling away again. It was a Friday morning and that night we were going to the New Forest for a drink, so I decided to tell her then.

The moment I told her she said,

"And I expect that you will be going to India after Cornwall, running away to see that bloody Indian holy man again".

She was more right than I cared to accept. We sat in silence for some time before deciding to return to the city. On the way, I asked her to stop so that we could talk.

I was using my job and India as an excuse to get out of the relationship and here was my chance to end it. It was a coward's way, but the only way I thought I had. When the car stopped I said,

"I think we should end our relationship".

Without hesitation she said,

"Yes, you're right".

As she said that, I was looking out the front of the car. My head swung round to her and I said,

"Let's get back together".

Inside my head, I could not believe what I was saying. I was shouting at myself within, "My God, what are you doing? She's letting you go. Shut up".

But I couldn't. I kept trying to get her to have me back. My head was reeling with thoughts, "Why do I immediately want her back? What's wrong with me?" Just 30 seconds ago when I was rejecting her, it was okay, but the moment I was being rejected I had to have her back. Why, when she no longer wanted me did I have to have her back?

Fortunately, she didn't have the same screwed up perspective of life as I had; she was stronger than I was. This time, no matter what I said, she had finally given up on me.

My mind replayed other events that were now obvious times I had done the same thing. For example, Christmas just a few years before, when at first I could not get a flight to India and was relieved that circumstances were not allowing me to go. Then I had a thought that maybe I was being rejected; I had to go, no matter what the cost. Other times I had walked away

Why?

from jobs, friendships, relationships; just about everything that needed commitment. When I was wanted, I had to run away.

My mind was reeling, trying to understand what it was about me that made me behave in such a stupid way.

It was obvious that I couldn't take being rejected. Even with Baba, he had never spoken to me or given me an interview, he, in a sense had never accepted me. By doing that I could not reject him, so I had to keep going back to India, subconsciously needing his acceptance.

Only when he accepted me would I have been free to run away. Baba had trapped me by using my own flawed character traits against me.

On Monday morning, I drove down to Cornwall for the new job, where I spent a month without a day off, but as the job neared the end I started to get agitated. The restlessness I had been feeling all year, started to become more intense. Again, I had to get away, but this time my contract was more binding, I could not just leave. As fate would have it, I managed to strain the arch in my foot, making standing or walking uncomfortable. I went to a doctor who said it would be ok in a day or two, but it was just the excuse I was looking for to get away.

It was now nearing the end of July and my birthday would be in a few days. I had hoped to celebrate it in the ashram. I managed to get a flight that arrived on the morning of the 28th.

Running Away Again

Just before I left the UK, an old friend from Australia, Ann, phoned to say that she was going to India, arriving 12 days after me and could I arrange accommodation and a taxi from the airport.

I would have Baba's Darshan on the afternoon of my birthday. I arrived in Puttaparthi in plenty of time to have a shower and change from my travelling clothes. I went to the token lines in what would normally be plenty of time, but as I neared the lines, it started to rain.

By the time I got to the token lines, I was too late, as the lines were already going in because of the rain. By the time I managed to enter the Darshan area, I was at the back of the hall and after the effort that I had made to get there, I was not a happy person at all.

When Baba did come out, I felt that I might as well have been on the moon. The feeling that I had turned a corner with Baba from the last trip was completely gone. Each Darshan after that, I ended up at the back of the hall, which, as the days went by, made me more and more agitated.

By the fourth day I had enough; the intensity of my feelings was just too much. I had to get away again. So I took the four-hour bus journey to Bangalore City, but even there I did not feel any better. I stayed for three days, hoping each day that the intensity I felt would ease or even stop, but even away from Baba, the feeling of stress would not go away.

Why?

So I returned again to the ashram, more out of the promise I had made to Ann, that I would meet her and arrange transport and a place for her to stay. All I really wanted to do was catch the next flight to the UK. Again, like so many other times, I felt trapped by circumstances.

When I reluctantly returned to the ashram, I realised that I had been expecting Baba to give me some attention. It was not a conscious thought; it was just there in the back of my mind. I should have known better — after all the years I had spent in the ashram, I had already learned that having expectations around Sai Baba invariably ended in pain.

Again, like many times before, I wrote him a letter, saying that I did not care for an interview or attention, I only needed him as a friend.

The following Darshan, I managed to get a place near the front. Baba took the letter and I calmed down a lot. By the time Ann arrived, I was much more at ease. We had been friends for six years, but now our friendship took a step closer. We decided to keep the relationship quiet, one reason being the cultural differences with the local Indians, plus some of the foreigners who live there have nothing better to do than gossip.

We had hardly been together 10 days, when the end of my trip was upon me. I could have stayed longer, but before going, I had promised my mother that I would visit her in Scotland. It had been almost a year since I had last seen her and to make sure I did go, I had purchased a flight ticket while still in the UK. Another reason I had done that was to make sure I did not extend my stay in India.

Some people enjoy going to Baba, then there is me. I know I need to go, but more often than not I enjoy leaving.

I had a nice week in Scotland with my mother and on my return to England I was wondering what to do next. I had not even been back in Liam's house more than 20 minutes, when the phone rang. It was Ann, wondering what I would be doing next. I told her I was just thinking the same thing and that I still had enough money left to go back to India. She had a better idea, "Why not come to Oz?"

It must have taken me all of five seconds to realise that this was by far a better idea than anything I was considering, so I decided to go. It was now late Tuesday afternoon, I still managed to book a flight for Thursday morning; the whole trip would last three weeks.

Ann took the Friday off work to pick me up from the airport, but she needn't have bothered. On my arrival at Heathrow, I was to find that the agents I purchased the tickets from had forgotten to send them to the airport. So after some hair pulling (mine not anyone else's), I would be delayed until the next flight, which would be ten hours after the one I was supposed to be on. As I was already three hours early, it was going to make for a very long day. About five hours into being bored, I started to wonder if the agent had booked me a veggie meal. I have always had problems getting the food that I request—especially with Gulf Air. So I thought it safer

Why?

just to check with the British Airways staff, and of course, the ticketing agents hadn't.

The staff at the British Airways counter were very helpful, but said it was a little too late to get a special meal, though they would give it a try. As the lady accessed her computer I said,

"Please, anything veggie but not a curry".

In spite of all the years I have spent in India, I still can't eat spicy foods, as I have found that flying and curry do not mix well for me.

It was now five o'clock and five hours till my new flight; the agents had still not turned up with the new ticket. After several phone calls, I managed to get a member of their staff. Unfortunately, she knew nothing about any tickets, but she would phone me back.

So I went back to tapping my fingers and trying not to think about what was happening. At 7:30 p.m. my tickets finally arrived with a very apologetic young woman. She handed me the folder with the ticket, which I checked. All the dates were in order, but there was no insurance certificate. The agent said,

"Don't worry, you won't need it".

Placated, I closed the folder, only to read on the front in bold letters: 'DON'T FORGET TO KEEP YOUR INSURANCE DOCUMENTS WITH YOU AT ALL TIMES'. I didn't say anything to her as I had already become resigned to the fact that this was just 'one of those days'.

I just lifted up the folder and pointed to her company's advice. She at least looked embarrassed, but there was nothing that could be done at that time of the night. At 10 o'clock, I was finally sitting on the aeroplane with everything I needed. I was hoping at this point that the worst was over. When the meal came round it was a curry; well at least I was on my way, so I settled down to watch the movie, only to find that the screen did not work either.

As an apology, the cabin staff gave me and the other two people beside me a bottle of wine each, which we all accepted graciously; even though at that moment a part of me wished I could drink something a little stronger.

When I arrived in Singapore, I found that my on-going flight to Perth would be delayed by three hours, then five, then seven. Through the night it slowly managed to rise to 14 hours. At last, 24 hours late, Perth. Australia, a place that as long as I could remember I had wanted to visit.

Ann met me at the airport and then we drove to her place in the hills just outside of the city. On the way, I told her what had happened over the last 48 hours and we had a good laugh about it all.

Ann lives in a beautiful area and one of the highlights of my stay was sitting on the veranda of her house on an evening looking at the stars. As there is almost no light pollution there, the heavens seemed brighter and vaster.

For the rest of the holiday, I had a great time seeing many of the sights in and around Perth and experiencing a way of life that seemed far more relaxed than in the UK.

It was not without some more problems though. At the end of the first week, Ann's car was broken into

Why?

when we were on the beach. Both of our bags and jeans that we had left on the back seat, along with my camera and watch, were stolen.

Then in the second week, I started to get some pain in my upper back. At first I took some painkillers, hoping that it would clear up on its own, but after a few days, Ann persuaded me to visit a chiropractor. After seeing him I went from taking some painkillers to chewing on them like sweets. By the end of the third week it was time to go, I had enjoyed the whole trip, especially the beach, where I managed to find that a fear I'd had of having my head under water was gone. I had not even noticed until after I had left the water.

On my return to the UK, I was just about out of money, in itself nothing new for me, only this time I had an injured back. I took the first job that came along, fitting out a yacht in Cornwall. After only three days I had to give it up, as the pain got worse, which was making me a little stressed out.

I was now getting quite worried. No money, no job and a bad back that gave no sign of getting better. I just kept holding on to the thought that everything is for a reason and Baba will supply what I need.

On the same day I returned to Southampton, Liam, my older brother, told me that I could start working with him fitting out the local swimming complex. I tried to explain (or make excuses) that my back was in too much pain and that I had left my tools in Cornwall. He had a good answer for everything I said and given that our other brother, Mick, would be the site foreman, I would be ok.

Running Away Again

The first job he gave me was fitting locks into ash doors. Luckily, the site manager liked my work, as he had been having some problems getting the finish he wanted. So I ended up just fitting locks all day every day, it allowed me to keep my back straight and the heaviest thing I had to lift was my hammer.

Unfortunately for me, my spate of bad luck was not yet over. After the first week, one of the men working on the scaffolding dropped a twelve-foot scaffolding pole just as I was walking past. It caught me a glancing blow on the muscle just above the left knee; an inch more and it would have easily shattered my leg.

It did cause me to do a rather strange little dance until I managed to find a wall to prop myself against. This time, no serious damage, although it was several months before I was able to bend my leg without discomfort.

Then, less than two weeks later, I was walking down some stairs, unfortunately I did not notice that the bottom one was not finished, so I fell over, twisting my ankle badly. I was taken to hospital again; nothing too serious, I just had to put some ice on it to stop the swelling and not walk on it too much.

Although I was told that I should take some time off, I decided against doing that, as I thought I needed the money. So the next day, I hobbled back into work.

A week later, Ann phoned saying that our relationship was over, we just lived too far apart. Then as if to top it off, the following morning I went over on the same ankle, exactly a week after I had done it the last time. I had stepped down into what would be one of the

Why?

children's play pools onto a piece of angled metal. As the area was in shadow, I did not see it, so I went over on the same ankle. This time it was far more painful and I had to be carried from the site.

Again, I had to visit the hospital, but this time the news was not so good. It could possibly take up to six weeks for it to be good enough to return to work. I found it hard to believe what had happened. Would my life always be full of these setbacks? I just kept thinking, is life really worth this shit?

The following week, I went to the doctors to check my ankle's progress, by the time I got to see the doctor I blurted out to him how I felt (taking me close to tears).

As I spoke to him, I realised I had been running away from everything for the last year—from work, relationships and especially from myself. I had not found any answer in or out of the ashram. Life had restrained me so much that I could not run anymore. The past year had finally caught up with me. It was stopping me dead and forcing me to experience a myriad of emotions that I had been avoiding since leaving the ashram in February. I asked the Doctor if I could see a counselor or psychiatrist. I hoped that a professional would help me to dig out the root cause of why I was feeling the way I was. Unfortunately, the counselors were fully booked for several months and the psychiatrist had a two-year waiting list. The doctor said he would keep trying. In the meantime, he offered me some drugs that he said would make me feel better. That was not a path I was happy to take. However I did feel relieved just to have been able to talk to someone.

Running Away Again

After I had been off for almost two weeks I was told that the company could no longer keep my position open. I was informed that if I did not return, they would have to fill the position. So even though the ankle was still painful, I bought a pair of high-legged boots, strapped my ankle up and returned to work.

A few days before my return to work, I had a dream of Baba. We were seated at a small table, leaning into it with our heads close together. Baba's hair touched my face making it tingle as if touched by a mild electric current. It felt wonderful, Swami then said to me,
"I want you to write your life story".

As he drew a small arrow on a piece of paper, he said,

"Write this much about your childhood".

Then as he drew a slightly larger arrow, he said,

"Write this much about the next part of your life".
Then as he drew a third arrow, which was longer again, he said,

"Write this much about the next part of your life".
Finally, he drew the largest arrow of all and said,

"Write this much about experiences you've had in the ashram".

On awakening, I could still feel the intense bliss within and knew that this somehow marked the end of what I had been going through over the past year.

I had no idea of how to start the longest thing I had ever written. My first attempt amounted to no more than three pages and that was on a small pad. How was I to write about all of my life?!

Why?

The first thing was to phone some friends from the Southampton bhajan group to ask if they would help. I told them of the dream and they agreed to help, and also had a spare Dictaphone that I could borrow.

When I went to fetch it, Steve (not Smith) said that he would also transcribe it for me. Even then I took my time starting it, as I felt very reluctant to begin. I managed to fill a tape before Christmas and returned it to Steve. After Christmas, I got another job in Cornwall refitting a ship, then I would probably go on to India after that. Steve told me he would transcribe it before I went. So I went to Cornwall on a new job on January 5. As I had become so aware of running away from things, I was determined to see this job through to the end. I would not run away again.

Everything went well and out of over 20 carpenters, I was one of the last two left to finish off the job. So I had proved, at least to myself, that I could see something through to the end without wanting to run away.

I even managed to write a page about some of my past. I went to India with the part that Steve had transcribed and the small piece that I had written. I took it into Darshan, although I expected nothing from Baba in the way of a blessing, as it was he who had told me to write it.

I also felt uncomfortable with the fact that I had not actually written it. I kept thinking about what Baba had said in the dream,

"I want you to write…"

By speaking into a Dictaphone and having someone else transcribe it didn't seem correct.

Running Away Again

So I started to write it myself. At first I was doing it in Darshan, but one day I had been writing about a difficult part of one of my stays in India. I just got so angry that by the time Baba came out, I was calling him about every expletive that I knew in the English language.

After Darshan, I went to have a coconut and considered what I felt and thought – resentment! I resented that the removal of the pain was in itself so painful.

There was nothing I could do but keep on going, so I returned to my room. I couldn't be bothered to write any more that day.

The next morning I could not find my notebook. Maybe I had left it at the coconut stand, but it was not there either and had not been handed in at the Lost and Found. I thought, "Oh well, I will have to start it again". I thought better of writing anything while waiting for Baba in the Darshan area, though.

The more I wrote, the more I started to have a deeper understanding of what had been happening to me. It was the healing of the mind and body. Yet, I learned that although so much had been healed, I had resented the way it had been done and had become very cynical about it and towards Sai Baba, who was the catalyst for what had being going on.

The part I wrote about started from when I first entered the ashram. I had to rewrite it so many times, the first time was mainly because I could not read my own handwriting, then to try and remove so many of the spelling mistakes. Doing the correcting again and again allowed me to see what had happened at a deeper level and I noticed more and more how much resentment I

Why?

felt towards the healing process. Everything around Baba seemed again to become more relaxed, the more I came to accept how the healing process had happened.

I was still going to Darshan every day, although the writing and thinking about my past took up most of my thoughts. On one occasion, when Sai Baba was walking around, he stopped to speak with some people. As I watched him, it seemed that although he was smiling, there was emptiness behind it, as if he was not really interested in that person he was talking to.

It had almost become automatic within me that when looked at others' behavior, that it must somehow be a reflection of my own.

My immediate thought was,

"No! I always pay attention to people when they speak to me".

As I left the Darshan area I had many conflicting thoughts. One that,

"It must be me" and another,

"I am sure that I am not like that".

By the time I had reached the coconut stall, I was ready to forget the whole line of thought. Just then, an Englishman approached me and started talking about his experiences with Baba,

"Baba takes over and writes the Bhajans through me, as writing something like that is beyond my abilities", he said.

I was smiling at him, but inside I was thinking, "Oh no, not again, why can't you see what you are capable of?"

Then it really hit home. I was being a hypocrite. This revelation came as a bit of a shock. I was doing one thing outside while doing something else inside.

I immediately started to give him my full attention, it no longer mattered that my views were different to his, it was what he believed that mattered and it was important to him. We talked on for another 30 minutes about his music and how Swami changed his life. By the time we had finished, I was beginning to enjoy the differences in how we both related to Sai Baba.

I was also lucky to be present at Shivaratri when Baba produced a Lingam (an egg-shaped representation of creation) in public for the first time in 28 years. I did not see it come out from his mouth; I saw it a few moments after it had been produced. I had been told if you see it at the point it emerges from an avatar's mouth, it is supposed to be your last life. But as I can't remember ever having a previous life, having another one doesn't really bother me.

On my return to the UK, the same employer as had hired me last time, offered me work in Liverpool. Again, I stayed on to the end of the job, doing that had become very important to me. At the end of the job I had enough money to go back to India, but I was trying to fight off the urge to do so. I felt I had been doing that far too much — finishing something then going back to Baba.

Instead, I went to Scotland to see my mother. While there, I hired a small car for a week and toured around my birthplace. It is amazingly beautiful! Looking over the River Clyde, on the far side there is a small range of

Why?

mountains. I sat a few times watching the sun go down. But the feeling to go to India would not leave me alone.

My brother Neil advised me to put my money into shares. So just to get the money in a place where I could not buy a flight ticket, I bought the shares.

After Scotland, I went to work in Germany. I stayed for five weeks on that job, doing 84 hours a week. By the time the job was over I was exhausted. Again, I had the money to return to India.

On my last visit, I had noted that Guru Poornima was going to fall on my birthday and I thought this would be a good time to go. It was now only the end of May, so I decided to go to Australia for five weeks, then on to India for only four weeks, mostly because I did not want to go to India for a long time again.

Over the months since the relationship had finished with Ann we had spoken every other week. Skipping around how we felt, never really letting go of each other, but not getting back together either. I knew it could not go on any longer; it had to finish, so that both of us could get on with our lives.

I also believed that a relationship other than just friends would not work. I was also thinking about my rejection-acceptance pattern and how that might be clouding my judgment. I knew I had to be doing this for the right reasons.

It took us a week to get around to how we both felt. We both decided that we could not be more than friends. It was not easy to get to that point for either of us, but we did manage to let go and we are still good friends.

Running Away Again

I then changed my dates so that I would only be staying in Australia for another week. On looking at my finances, I realised I could not afford to stay there for another four weeks.

When I arrived in India, Baba was in Kadugodi, Bangalore, so I took a 40-minute taxi ride to the ashram. I did not expect anything and I was not let down. Baba then went to Puttaparthi the following day. I stayed on in Bangalore for a few days, as I was not in a hurry to be around Baba or the ashram. When I did arrive in Puttaparthi, I felt that I did not need to be there anymore, that I was over the feelings of rejection.

I did not need to be accepted, I could leave anytime. It was an immense feeling of freedom, I didn't need to stay around there and be ignored.

An old memory flashed in front of me of what I thought was my first love. She had rejected me before I had rejected her. It was strange to understand that missing her so much had all been a lie. I had never loved her, my mind had only clung to the feeling of rejection, confusing it with what I thought was love and now I realised that I had probably never really loved anyone. I pushed the thoughts aside, not wanting to dwell on them.

The following morning was my first Darshan, and I got a front row seat, which was very pleasant.

At night, there would not be a normal Darshan, but bhajans in the Poornachandra Hall (opposite the main Darshan area), because of work being carried out in the Mandir. So I skipped that, just going to the hall at the very end of the bhajans.

Why?

The next morning, I again had a front row. Just before Baba came out, I started thinking that now there was no reason for him not to speak to me. As he came near I started to panic, then for a moment he was standing directly in front of me, maybe he would! But by then, I was plain scared. Looking at him up and down, I was not able to keep my eyes in the same place. I was relieved that he ignored me and had just walked past. I did wonder why I had reacted in that way.

The following morning, I got another front row and Baba kept his back to me as he passed, without even looking in my general direction. This I was used to, so that was not a problem for me and in some way I felt relieved.

That evening, Baba was doing bhajans in the Poornachandra Hall again, so I stood outside talking to a friend. At the end of bhajans, Baba started to walk off the platform area, moving in our direction, so from the outside I gave him a cheeky wave and said, Bye Swami.

Just at that moment, he stopped dead. I thought he was going to wave back at me. Even though I was 200 metres away, again I was scared.

Too many things like this had happened over the last few days to pass as coincidence, so I started in earnest to try and understand what was happening. It didn't take me long and it was quite simple, I was afraid of the commitment, of being accepted; I was afraid of being loved. Acceptance and rejection – two sides of the same coin. I had stood up to my fear of rejection, now I had to stand up to my fear of being accepted, it was so obvious. Acceptance and rejection were the Yin and Yang of pain.

If I suffered from one, I suffered from the other. Now I could not leave, I had gone through so much; this small thing had to be resolved.

I missed Darshan the next morning, but learnt that Sai Baba had gone out to visit his students in one of the colleges. So I walked along that road in the hope of seeing him, at the same time wondering how he was going to get me over this fear.

Sometime later, his car came past. I could see him waving to people. As he came to me he turned away. That single act convinced me that the only way around this was to stand up and demand to be noticed, to say, "Hey! I am here! I demand to be noticed".

Over the next few days, I had several front row seats and each time I would get myself mentally ready to get up on my knees and ask for an interview. Over the years, I had asked him many times only to be ignored, but had never got up onto my knees, as I didn't want to be noticed that much and I had a great excuse for not trying that hard. I didn't want to spoil other people's view that sat behind me. Now it seemed the only way forward.

Each time he came close to me, Baba would pass on the other side keeping his back to me. This now only made me more determined to try again and again.

Through this, I was now beginning to understand the feelings of rejection from my mother. She had told me many times as a child that I was always so quiet. What she didn't understand was that as I sat in the house every night, I was in fact hiding. If no one noticed

Why?

me, then no one could hurt me. She just did not see what I was doing.

I was beginning to think that what I had been doing around Darshan was similar to my childhood. I had to now force myself to stand up and know that I deserved to be noticed.

By July 3rd I had been there for ten days and had been getting front row seats almost every day, always trying to get close to Baba to speak to him, but so far unsuccessfully. I had always said to people,

"I would rather be ignored in the front row than at the back".

And this is what was happening to me and yes it was a lot easier. Finally he was coming my way, he came the closest to me since I had decided that he should notice, he had got to just 6-10 feet away. I knew if I waited for him to come closer, he would turn and walk away. So I raised myself onto one knee and said loudly,

"Interview".

He looked me straight in the eyes and said,
"Yes!"

A tingling sensation seemed to wash though the body. Stunned, I then sat back down. That was not the answer I was expecting; my mind went blank as I watched Baba as he continued walking. It was a short time before the mind started to form any thoughts and by then Baba was quite some distance away, even then, there was nothing in me that wanted to do anything.

It was only as he was on the veranda that I thought,
"He said yes and I did not get up".

Running Away Again

I wasn't going to tell anyone about this, how could I explain it! he had finally said "Yes" and I couldn't get up, Why?

I had seen hundreds of groups go for an interview — many times seeing one group member having to be pulled onto their feet by their friends. Had I become so used to others helping, that I couldn't start things on my own? Was it that I felt I needed to have the support of others? I knew that I had to find the strength within to get up myself.

Darshan had finished and as I stood up, my decision not to tell only one came to a very abrupt end; an American I had know for years was beside me and I couldn't keep it to myself.

"George, promise me you won't tell anyone what I am about to say".

He smiled,

"Yeah Joe".

"I just asked Baba for an interview and he said, "Yes".

"Did he say Go?"

"No."

"Well he was only saying you would get an interview. If he didn't say 'go', you could have to wait another ten years or more for it."

Most of what he said was lost to me, because as I was telling him, I felt a rush of energy leave my body. It started from low down and felt like a wave as it washed upwards. As it got to my head, I felt the emotions for only a second and then it was over, leaving me feeling light headed.

Why?

It was the same tingling sensation I had felt back in '93 Shivaratri when an old energy left the body through the head, but more intense.

I understood later, that as I was telling George, what had happened was in some way me accepting Sai Baba and some emotional energy that had stopped me getting on with living life had left the body. So I thought I should tell everyone I knew, but in the back of my mind there was still some regret that I had foregone the opportunity to speak to Baba. The next few days I tried to speak to Baba again before I went of to Bangalore, but I was not getting anywhere near him.

I needed to see a dentist and Sam my Canadian friend was leaving India, so we both went to a nice hotel for the night, then went to a bar. I hadn't had a drink for almost seven years and had become tired of telling people,

"I haven't had a drink for one year"

"I haven't had a drink for two years".

As each year passed, I would add another number. I had become fed up of telling people, so I had decided that I would be having a couple of drinks that evening. Seven years without an alcoholic drink is such a long time, that after only four drinks, I knew that I had already passed my limit (a bit of a difference from when I could drink a bottle). Then we went and had a pizza.

As we walked to the pizza shop, I was amazed at how much my perceptions had been changed by the alcohol. People passing by seemed to be unreal, it was almost as if I was watching a movie that was too bright and a bit wobbly. I know it was the alcohol doing it, but still I found it fascinating to watch. I had a really great time and we both laughed about some of the stupid things we had got up to in the past. The next morning though was not so interesting, as I was suffering badly from dehydration, more commonly referred to as a hangover. I did though have a sense of relief, I could no longer tell people how long it had been since I had had a drink, as I knew a part of me had been using it to say,

"Hey, look how good I have been".

My first Darshan on returning to the ashram was a bit of a shock. Baba was just about finished Darshan and was on the veranda when a man climbed on to the veranda at the opposite end to Baba. He was holding his chest and leaning to one side, seeming to be in some distress, his walking was also erratic. As I watched, I actually thought, "He looks as if he's dying".

I watched him intently until he went out of sight near the area where you would go into the interview room. Then a few moments later, he came back into view still heading towards Baba, but now he was flailing his arms around in the air. He was obviously in some kind of emotional distress.

The security managed to stop him about three feet away from Baba. He tried to push them off so he could get nearer. It was obvious that he did not want to harm Baba deliberately, but he did look as if he was going to throw himself around him.

The security had to force him away. I had seen several events like this in the past and they had always jolted me emotionally. I guess I have seen it happen four or five times over the years. The first time, the jolt of

Why?

watching it left me feeling depressed for several days. The second time the same; the third time less; now I had a different perception of what was going on when these events took place. Baba used them to draw out the negative energy from people in the crowd. This time was no exception for me, as I felt a momentary feeling of dread rise up within, then almost as quickly leave the body within moments of it all happening.

Watching him being pulled off the veranda did make me re-evaluate any plans I may have made in the future about simply walking in again for an interview.

A few Darshans later, I was sitting in the second row when Baba came past. He was nearer than the last time I had triad to talk to him, so I got up on my knee again and asked,

"Swami, interview please".

Again he looked me in the eye and said,

"Where do you come from?"

He said it so softly that I was about to say, "Pardon?" But I had heard what he said inside.

"Scotland", I said loudly.

As we looked at each other, I felt as if I was focusing on him for the first time. He then turned and walked on, so I sat back down, and immediately thought,

"No, Get up, get up!"

I stood up with every intention of going to the interview room. Baba turned back when I had stood and he said very gently,

"Sit down. Sit down".

It took about five minutes for my heart to stop racing. When it did, I felt completely normal, so normal in fact that maybe it was a bit boring, but I had done it. I had found the strength to stand up and the body had felt no fear.

Several days later, I had a dream of Sai Baba. In it, I ran up to him meaning to ask for an interview,

"Baba can I have your Darshan?"

"You can have my Darshan, but an interview is not good for your growth at this time."

As he said the last word, I woke and was not too happy, although I still believed that at some time in the future, Baba would give me an interview. After all, he had said to me in Darshan, "Yes". So it was only a matter of time.

Since the beginning of this trip, I had sometimes been hanging out with a young American, by the name of Pete. He had rented a flat next to mine, just outside the ashram. I noticed him one day with an older American whom I had been avoiding for years. No matter how hard I tried, I was always very uncomfortable around him. He lived permanently in India, making his money from other foreigners by channeling energy, which in itself I did not like, and he seemed to have an unusual relationship with a young Indian 'helper', which even to a casual observer, was obviously more than just friendship. I told Pete what I thought of the healer and his relationship.

This led Pete to back away from the older American. Then several days later he told me that when he was 10 years old an older man had sexually abused him, which then went on for quite some time. He asked me what he

Why?

should do if the healer tried to put his arm around him again. The only thing I could think to say was,

'The next time he tries to put his arm around you, just say, "NO, don't do that", then walk away. Pete did not bring him up in conversation again, so I though that was the end of that. Although over the next few days we spent a lot of time walking around talking, sometimes he would touch on his past. I had set one rule to our conversations, 'no talking about spirituality'. We came across the older American a few times, but as casually as we could, we headed off in another direction, easily managing to avoid him.

It was now only two days since the dream of Baba, when the shit hit the fan, big style! That morning, when I was sitting in the back of the Darshan area meditating as I waited on Baba, a realisation suddenly popped into my head. The older American man was about to accuse me of being gay. Dismayed, I thought, "Well, I will just have to deal with it when or if it happens".

After Darshan, I went to the western canteen in the ashram. Just before the doors were about to open, Pete came up to me and said,

"I saw him this morning and I was just going to say 'NO', but before I could, he said,

"It's not me that's gay, its Joe, and I'm going to confront him about it later".

As I had been expecting it, the news came as no surprise. I just felt a little more dismayed than I had earlier.

"It's OK Pete."

I was resigned to the fact that this was something I had to go through. So, I went into the canteen and started breakfast as normal. Soon afterwards, the older man arrived and came straight to the table that I was sitting at.

A rather one-sided argument ensued, in which he accused me, very loudly, of being gay and liking young men. During all this time, I had a searing sensation in my head and I do not remember all that was said, but in the end I was happy that I had managed to reply to his remarks without anger. And, as a whole, I simply let him get on with what he wanted to say. In the back of my mind I knew this was all related to the dream and what Baba had said,

"An interview is not good for your growth at this time".

When he finished venting his feelings, he left with his little group of friends and I finished my breakfast, deliberately taking my time, then went back to my room, still with the searing sensation going on in my head.

When I got back to my room, I looked at how I felt about what I had been accused of. I wasn't that concerned, but the more time I spent alone, the more I became pissed off at Baba, as it seemed that this whole situation had been orchestrated and I was fed up with being in a place where I was constantly being forced into emotional situations.

The more I thought about it, the angrier I became. I just wanted to leave this sodding place, but I thought that now I could not. I knew if I left, it would mean that people might believe the older man and when I returned sometime in the future, I would have to deal

Why?

with this all over again and maybe by then it would be worse. Leaving or staying I was left with a sense of being unjustly accused that would not go away.

However, it was not the memories of what had just happened that kept returning but that of Benny McKay, from my childhood; particularly the time he was ranting and raving with the knife and with that came emotions of fear as well as anger at being so trapped.

I kept trying to push these memories and feelings away. I was having a bad enough time dealing with what had just happened, but memories surfaced of occasions in my past when Benny had been accusing and punishing me for things I had not done, but not just the memories, the feelings that went with them too. They seemed to burn my mind; I then noticed for the first time that Benny McKay and this older man, who had made the accusations, looked so alike that they could easily pass as brothers. By late afternoon, I was beginning to wonder if this was all about that pain being released.

Had I subconsciously transferred all my dislikes to this man? Was I blaming him for some of the things that had happened to me? I didn't know. I was just bloody confused. All I wanted was the feelings to stop.

By the following day I decided that I should apologise. I knew that I was wrong to have judged him in the first place to Pete, although that judgment had gone on in my mind for several years, but first I would tell Pete what I was going to do and why.

When I met him and explained what had been going on he said to me,

"You don't understand. I had not said anything to him. He just approached me and said those things about you. It was after that, that I said, "NO. Go away!"

This had some bad implications. If he had said it after Pete had said 'no go way', then I could accept that he would have made his accusations about me as a self-defense. This made things different. How could the Benny McKay look-alike have known Pete and I had been talking about him or why we had been avoiding him? It wasn't as if it was obvious, Puttaparthi is a big place. He could not have known, so why then had he jumped to the conclusion that I thought he was gay! What was his accusation about if not that! I now felt that it had become impossible to apologise. What would I be apologising for! This meant that I had to carry on with the pain I felt inside.

I had hoped that if I apologised, the pain I felt would go away. Over the next few days I avoided almost everyone I knew in the ashram, but eventually I decided, right or wrong, that I should never have allowed a situation like this to even start. There was a very good chance that I was completely wrong about this person.

I would explain to the older American what I experienced since our argument and apologise, not for what we had said, but for how I had always disliked him because he had reminded me so much of Benny McKay.

He listened and accepted what I said, but that still did not stop the feelings I had inside. As for the rest of my trip, a part of me seemed to curl up and hide, as I was plagued with a very deep sense of sadness, although I didn't know then, that this experience had

Why?

dragged up from within me the same feeling I had the day I saw Benny MacKay in the club when I was 19 years old. I thought I felt the sadness for him, but I hadn't. Seeing him had merely drawn out the sadness that had been hiding within me from when I was a child and this incident at the ashram had caused it to surface again. Now it did not go away. I was not even aware of how deeply it was affecting me until my next trip to India.

Chapter Eleven

This Is Your Biggest Change

On my return to the UK, I was surprised to find that the shares I bought in March had almost doubled, so at least something was looking up. I hoped to work straight through till at least May of the next year, so I started looking for a job. Over the next six weeks, I only managed to get thirteen working days; eight days on one job then five on another. Both jobs were about to finish, so it was easy to see them through to the end.

I did a lot of walking around and thinking, mostly to combat getting bored as I tried not to dwell on the constant pull to return to India. Emotionally I seemed to have been reset to when I was a teenager, where smiling was difficult. That, with no work and a dwindling bank balance also did not help. I had hoped for one job in particular on the ships, but that was not due to start till mid-September, but there was not even a definite date, everything else I was being offered I needed a car for.

Instead of leaving the shares and allowing them to continue growing, I decided to cash them in and buy a little second hand car to make it easier to get a job. I sold

Why?

them on Thursday and was told the money would be in my bank account in five working days. The next few days, I was deeply conflicted, I needed a car and a job, but no matter how I looked at the world around me, I felt no happiness with being a part of it. I was alone every day, at least in the ashram I could be around some like-minded people.

By Monday morning I had decided to go to India again, as it was by far my biggest pull. Reluctantly I bought a ticket and I would arrive in India on 16th September. The first day I stayed in Bangalore, again I had no desire to rush to Baba's ashram, so I did a lot of window shopping, trying to delay the inevitable. When I did go to Puttaparthi, I was not at all happy. By coming, I thought that I had given up a chance to settle. I had for a while been doing well, now I was spending the little money I did have on being in Sai Baba's ashram yet again.

I had become afraid of being happy, as each time I had managed to get out of a dark place; there was always something that dragged me back down. I also started to think of myself as some sort of emotional junkie, that there would always be something to dig up from my past and wondered what it would be next.

There would be another Paduka ceremony and I would not be involved. I would really rather have someone drill a hole in my teeth than just sitting watching it. So I made a phone call to Bangalore and made an appointment on the date of the ceremony. No more than 30 minutes after I had made the appointment, Sylvester,

This Is Your Biggest Change

an Englishman I knew who lived in America, asked me if I would be someone's partner during the Puja.

I so wanted to say no, but I remembered the effect it had on me two years ago, so like the last time, I changed my dates and stayed for the ceremony. I was hoping that the sense of sadness I was still experiencing would be healed.

I did experience the tingling sensation that I've come to realise is an emotional energy leaving the body, but afterwards my mind still did not become any more peaceful or happy. It was really at this point that I noticed what had been going on for months. I was finding it really difficult to smile; my face had become like a man who played card games for money, it showed nothing of what was going on inside and that was how my inside felt as well; nothing, empty.

A week after the Puja, I was sitting beside Sylvester in Darshan. Most of his group had returned to America, so there was just him and his wife.

"When Baba comes past, I will say three for interview, Baba", said Sylvester.

"OK, but if he asks, How many? Two? Then just you and Clare go."

But really, I was just being polite.

When Baba came past us I stretched as far as I could with a letter, but Baba just walked around me. Then I heard Sylvester say.

"Swami, three for interview."

"How many?"

"Three, Swami."

Then to my surprise, Baba said,

Why?

"Go".

And I was off.

As I walked up to the veranda, I felt that my heart was trying to kick a hole in my chest. I looked down at my shirt to see the front of it bouncing out with the beat of my heart. I reached the veranda and looked around, Sylvester was only just beginning to stand up. Someone pointed to an empty space, so I sat down, then Sylvester and Clare appeared.

A few minutes later, Baba came into view. As he came onto the veranda, he let out a large,

"Ooooh", raising his eyebrows as if he was surprised to see someone. If I was not so nervous, I might otherwise have laughed, as it was quite comical.

As he walked past me, I was half expecting him to say,

"What are you doing here?"

But he passed by, going to a small group of Indians behind me, speaking briefly to them before turning and going into the interview room. A few moments later, he appeared in front of me at the doorway and without looking at me, he flicked his finger to indicate that we should go into the interview room.

It wasn't till the moment I stepped past the door itself that I really believed it was going to happen.

When we were inside, Sylvester and Clare sat directly in front of Swami's chair. I was just to the right of it and was about to sit, when I noticed that the Indians who had entered behind us were all still standing. I was half way back up when Baba entered saying, "Cootcho, Cootcho",

This Is Your Biggest Change

Telegu for sit down. With a wave of his hand, Baba started to produce Vibhuti, which he gave to the two Indian ladies. Then, as he gave it to Clare, he pushed it into the palm of her hand saying,

"This is Prashanti Nilayam".

Clare replied,

"The abode of highest peace".

Then he gave some to Sylvester, who then turned and tried to give me some, but I was trying to indicate to him that Baba was not finished. He seemed to understand and turned back to Baba, who asked him,

"Where is God?"

"Everywhere Baba", Sylvester replied.

"Are you sure?"

"Yes, Baba."

"How do you know?"

This seemed to fluster him for the briefest of moments. He then said,

"Faith, Baba, I have faith".

Then Baba gave him a light slap on the cheek and sat down.

He took Sylvester's hand and started to play with his ring, which Baba had given him 12 years before. As he was playing with it he was saying,

"So small, so small".

I looked over the arm of Baba's chair with a frown, because Sylvester's ring is about the biggest one I've ever seen, taking up almost the entire first knuckle of his finger and partly covering the finger on either side. It's more like a small plate than a ring.

Then Baba said,

Why?

"How is your wife?"

"Very good, Swami. Thank you, she is a very good woman."

Then Baba turned to Clare and said,

"How is your husband?"

"He is a very good man, Swami. Thank you."

Then Swami said,

"Yes, very good man. Why do you argue with him?"

At that, Clare got a bit flustered.

"Why do you argue?"

I thought Clare was about to cry.

Then Baba turned to his right and talking over my head, started to speak to an Indian politician who was behind me. First he said something in an Indian language and the politician replied in that language as well.

Then Baba said in English,

"This is your biggest change".

Then he resumed the conversation in the Indian language.

I was left wondering whether the English message was meant for me, but I dismissed it, as almost all the changes I had gone through consisted of a lot of pain and tears.

Baba then spoke to one other Indian in his own language. Then he indicated for him to come closer. Because of where I was sitting I had to move to the back wall to allow him to get near Baba.

Baba again spoke to him in an Indian language, then started to wave his hand and produced a nine-planet ring. He then turned to Sylvester and said,

This Is Your Biggest Change

"Go inside".

Sylvester stood without picking up the cushion he was sitting on, but Clare picked it up for him and then went into the private interview room. Baba then said, "See, that is duty", referring to Clare picking up her husbands cushion. Then he followed them in.

About 10 minutes later they came out and Baba turned to Clare saying,

"Do you like green?"

"Yes, Swami."

He then waved his right hand and produced a large green diamond ring for her and placed it on her finger.

Next, Baba told the politician to go in with his son. They were also in for about 10 minutes, and as they came out Swami indicated for the other four Indians, two men and two women, to go inside.

I was feeling a little bemused, maybe he will be giving me a private interview on my own and then maybe he won't, so I sat mentally twiddling my thumbs. About 10 minutes later, the door opened again and my chest leapt in anticipation, thinking, "It's my turn now", but Baba seemed to rush past me, heading towards the door that led out of the interview room. Surprised, I said,

"SWAMI?"

He glanced down at me, but still headed towards the door, opening it and indicating that everyone should leave.

By now the other Indians had come out of the private interview room and were standing between the main door and where I was seated in stunned disbelief. Not only had Sai Baba interacted with everyone else in

Why?

the room, but the position of the three Indians and the lad seemed to be designed specifically to show me what Swami had created for them. The three of them had their hands in a prayer like manner, one low, one in the middle and one at a higher position. As I looked I could clearly see that all three of them were now wearing the nine-planet rings. In India the ring is supposedly a talisman that wards off the negative astrological influence of the 9 planets. And, as if to pour some salt into my wounds, Baba grabbed the politician's son's arm, pulled it out so it was clearly in my line of sight and there, hanging from his wrist was a new watch. A very large new watch! Baba was smiling, looking at it and while I couldn't hear him, I just knew that he was asking him if he liked it. It was obvious that the boy was very pleased, as he was nodding his head in an exaggerated manner. He was no doubt saying, "Yes! Yes".

Everyone started to go outside, so I tried to leave last, not really believing that it was over. I still had the letter, so I decided that as I passed Baba at the door I would hand him the letter and say,

"Will you speak with me?"

As I passed him, I handed him the letter saying, "Will you speak..."

"I will speak. I will speak", said Baba before I had managed to say "with me". And before I knew it, Baba was gone, the door had closed behind me and I was outside the interview room walking away wondering what had just happened!

The strangest thing was that I felt fine. I wasn't angry or jealous. I asked myself, "How do I feel?" Normal,

This Is Your Biggest Change

I felt normal. I just did not understand what, if anything, had just happened. And as to Baba saying,

"I will speak. I will speak".

Well, he seemed to be a little evasive, he didn't say, "I will speak to YOU".

As I walked off the veranda, someone approached me, I could only put my hand out and shake my head "No", I was not yet ready to talk.

Sylvester invited me to his room for some tea and the three of us spoke about what had just happened, or in my case what didn't happen. I did feel that something in my mind had changed — but what?

As I left Sylvester's room, I tried to avoid anyone that I knew, a lot of people knew that I had been coming to the ashram for a long time and that I had not got an interview, and right now I wasn't quite sure how to explain what had happened.

When I was talking to Sylvester, I realised that it was just over seven and a half years since I first arrived and I had lived around Baba's ashram for three of those years.

Over the next few days, I started to understand some of the things that took place; everything that Baba had done should have upset me emotionally — giving others jewellery, speaking to everyone and then taking them all into the private interview room, but none of it affected me at all. It was like he was replaying the events of my childhood – my brothers and sister getting attention, being given things and me having to move out of the way for them, but this time there was no pain, no jealously and no anger.

Why?

Something in my mind had just changed; it was more at peace.

The feelings I experienced as a child were no longer there. Immediately after the interview, I was just happy.

The deep feeling of sadness that I had gone into the interview with was simply gone.

I thought a lot about what Baba had said,

"This is your biggest change".

I looked at how he had cured me of the alcohol and the cigarettes.

If it had not been that I was drinking a bottle each time I had a drink, I would not even have noticed a change had taken place. It was so natural to no longer drink and also the cigarettes were the same. I had smoked 20-30 every day for 10 years. Then the addiction was simply gone.

Again, the change was so natural that on reflection, I know that I would not even have noticed that the change had happened but for the fact of the addiction being so obvious. The sadness I was going through before the interview was also simply gone.

It's been several years since the interview and I feel that I am still 'growing into' whatever had happened in that short time. I am a much happier person than I've ever been even in the most difficult of times. Though life still throws up challenges, I still try to meet it head on.

It has taken me a long time to understand that the first letter I wrote to Sai Baba was the one of greatest importance. In it I asked, "Who am I?" I can't say I fully understand, but I have been fortunate enough to glimpse divinity within, to see a beauty in creation that I never knew existed. I can understand the pain within myself and that the experiences I've had around the ashrams were the taking away of who I am not and of course, when the pain is taken away, what is left is happiness.

    I understand that I will continue to make mistakes in life, but what I was given in the ashrams and continue to be given, is a balance in my life.

    As the whirlwind off life happens around me, I am still left with a peace within. I may lose it momentarily, in the most difficult of times, but nothing is ever as bad as it was before coming to Sai Baba.

    I still travel to India every year (Except 2004 for medical reasons) and have continued to grow as a person. For as long as I can remember all I ever wanted was to be a better person and I will be forever grateful to Sai Baba for being the catalyst that caused so much needed change.

2015. I have now been married for 11 years (I met Ying thirteen years ago) and have three children; Kayleigh 10, Sing 17 and Dodo 25, all girls. I never thought life would be quite this different.